Colorful
Knitwear
Design

from *Threads*

W9-BAA-017

Colorful Knitwear Design

from *Threads*

The Taunton Press

Cover photo by Susan Kahn

Taunton
BOOKS & VIDEOS
for fellow enthusiasts

© 1994 by The Taunton Press, Inc.
All rights reserved.

First printing: June 1994
Second printing: January 1995
Printed in the United States of America

A THREADS Book

THREADS® is a trademark of The Taunton Press, Inc.,
registered in the U.S. Patent and Trademark Office.

The Taunton Press
63 South Main Street
Box 5506
Newtown, CT 06470-5506

Library of Congress Cataloging-in-Publication Data

Colorful knitwear design / from Threads.
    p. cm.
  "A Threads book" — T.p. verso
  Includes index.
  ISBN 1-56158-082-1
  1. Sweaters. 2. Knitting. I. Threads magazine
TT825.C647 1994   94-4639
746.9'2 — dc20   CIP

Contents

Introduction

Knitting a sweater can seem to present some overwhelming choices. First there's the fiber to pick, then the color or maybe the texture, and finally the finishing technique. Well, here's expert help from the pages of *Threads* magazine to guide you through the maze of decisions.

Whether you need advice on how to decide on a harmonious color scheme, whether you've chosen to work with alpaca or mohair, or whether you're charting lace or multicolor patterns, you'll find practical information within for making just the sweater you're coveting. From creative construction—making a sweater with strips of knit, forming fabric from blocks of different textured patterns—to custom embroidered embellishment and beautified borders, the expertise offered in the following pages will get you into a knit that fits and flatters.

Amy T. Yanagi, editor

At Play in the Land of Color

Finding fortuitous combinations for vibrant knitting

by Dorothy Bird

Dorothy Bird's memories of afternoon tea with her mother's good china, and careful observation of the pattern inspired the color choices for her sweater "Royal Albert."

t his is for people who love color—pale color, saturated color, color combinations, color that sings. It's about a few ways I've found to translate that response into personal work, especially into designs for knitting. Designers who use color need to know how to look, where to look, and how to interpret and apply what they see. In other words, how, as Josef Albers said in his book, *The Interaction of Color* (Yale University Press, 1975), "to develop—through experience—by trial and error—an eye for color."

Starting with the colors themselves

As designers, I think we must learn to pay closer attention to the colors that stimulate us in our environment, in nature, and in art. I consciously focus on colors that draw my eye and notice how they change in relation to other colors. I like to select one color family, green for instance, and pay particular attention to that color for an extended period. While "thinking green," I look for it in all of its glorious forms, the pale celedons of Chinese porcelain, the darkly intense bottle greens, chartreuse, sage, khaki, turquoise, the spectrum of greens found in a spring garden. I look at adjoining colors and how they affect green and then ask myself what works, what doesn't, and why? Then I try translating my observations and discoveries into yarn choices, and ultimately into a project, something knitted.

Harmonies

Sometimes, I select a particular color and see where it takes me. For example, I once explored that elusive color between brown and purple. I collected yarns, lights and darks, and wove a coat, with knitted sleeves, alternating the colors that tended toward brown with those that thought they were purple. I called the coat "When is a plum a prune?"

Another approach is to select two different colors and then fill in the gap, making a transition from one to the other, graduating through the spectrum. By including warm and cool or bright and pale colors within the transition, graduated compositions can be very stimulating, even within a limited range.

Discords

Many years ago I took a basic design class on color. I've never forgotten one particular assignment. We were to select the four colors that we thought "clashed," the worst color combination imaginable. Then we were to combine these four into a geometric pattern, like a tile or quilt block, and repeat it 12 times on a large piece of paper.

I chose pink, turquoise, avocado, and gold (my mother had just installed a turquoise range and refrigerator). When the class's completed assignments were displayed, they turned out to be unexpectedly beautiful, and we all learned about being hampered by color preconceptions.

Remembering recently the rich parfait of color I had assembled for that class, I decided to knit it. I started out with the four original colors, using my standard method: I collected the colors, along with a variety of shades, and laid them in a basket placed in a well-travelled location. As I passed the basket, I added or removed colors or changed texture by adding mohair, silk, angora, etc. I call this process "percolating." Then one day the basket of colors waved its little arms and said, "It's time to start!" You can see what I wound up with in the photo on p. 11; there were about 60 colors in the collection before I was through; I call it "Color 101."

Starting with inspiring objects

When recalling fond memories, I often recall key elements that made an important visual impression on me. As I was growing up, on special occasions, my mother served tea using her "Royal Albert" tea set. She had a pattern that she'd first received as a wedding present in 1934, known generically as an "Imari" pattern. It was a loosely translated Japanese design in cobalt, rust, and gold leaf, on white porcelain. I was visiting her again, after I had learned to look at objects in terms of color, and she served tea using that tea set. I looked at the colors and thought fiber. To the white/rust/cobalt/gold I added burgundy/eggplant/black. I eventually had 25 yarns within those color parameters, including a brassy gold viscose for the gold leaf. After experimenting with graphing out some of the tea set patterns, I selected a few designs that fell somewhere between Imari and what I call the Great Fair Isle Collective Unconscious.

I wanted the colors to gradually metamorphose from one to another, so I knitted every row with two strands of yarn, which allowed me to knit as follows: one row with two strands of color A, a row with one strand each of color A and color B, a row with two strands of color B, a row with one strand of color B and one of color C, etc. And so Royal Albert changed from porcelain to fiber. ⇨

Analyzing the colors in a variegated, tweedy yarn led to the yoke design for the sweater "Yellow Orange" above. A length of decorative trim suggested the South of France and prompted the collection of yarns below, destined for a sweater called "Provençe."

A favorite Kilim rug, wisely photographed before the shop sold it, provided both pattern and color inspiration for Bird's "Kilim Coat."

Yarns

What could be more invigorating to a knitter than a well-stocked yarn store? Besides the obvious allure of those beautifully colored solid yarns, the vast array of tweeds and variegated yarns available today offers color inspirations that are easily accessible. I recently used a bulky tweed yarn that was basically a medium cool grey with small flecks of white, pink, lavender, light blue, and an intense blue-green. Picking up any of the first four colors would have produced a nice enough sweater, but combining the tweed with another yarn in that unusual blue-green resulted in something entirely different.

I enjoyed the process so much that I did a second sweater using a yellow-orange tweed with white, orange, and pale blue flecks, picking up all three colors; it's shown on p. 9. While wearing these sweaters, I was once again reminded that the more unusual a sweater is, the more readily people recognize it as handmade. Be experimental. Your sweater is going to be individually created, stitch by stitch, and it might as well be recognized as such. Exciting color selection is the easiest way to accomplish this.

Fabric

Fabric stores can provide equally inspiring color combinations; don't neglect the stores that specialize in interiors and upholstery. For the "percolation" mixture on p. 9, I was inspired by a length of ribbon trim from Pierre Deux (870 Madison Ave., New York, NY 10021 and 17 other locations). This fabric store specializes in cotton and challis that's imported from Provençe, in southern France. The designs of flower motifs and the border prints capture the essence of summer, the sweet smells and warm breeezes found in sundrenched meadows and in gardens spilling over with flowers. The border print that I chose to epitomize those characteristics contains an especially interesting color combination.

Textiles

I love to look at fabric and rugs from the Middle East, Eastern Europe, Africa, Asia, South America, wherever there are textiles that are stimulating sources for new ideas. Oasis, a favorite shop of mine in Seattle, has a wonderful collection of antique Middle Eastern rugs.

The owner willingly talks about history, weaving techniques, and any other pertinent information, while rolling out one example after another as illustrations. An old slit-tapestry Kilim from the Caucasus caught my attention several years ago. On a white background were bold medallions in shades of grey-green, rusty orange, and

Recollecting a college art assignment to compose with her least favorite colors inspired Bird's latest effort, "Color 101." She started with a basketful of incompatible colors and added elements gradually until the mix worked.

blue-blacks. I was so attracted to the colors and designs that each time I visited the store I would find it, unroll it, and gaze longingly. I took several photographs of it. Alas, someone else had the audacity to buy "my" rug. After a period of self-recrimination, I decided that since I couldn't have the original, I would knit it. And I had the photographs! While graphing out the medallions, I realized that they would be so large that the only proper garment to knit would be a coat; you can see "Kilim Coat" in the photo at left.

The advantage of yardage swatches and photos is that they are portable and can be taken to the yarn stores for color matching. I scour books and magazines for good photographs and I look closely at the photos, samples, and swatches I collect. In addition to the obvious colors that make up the designs, very often there are small bits of color that don't dominate the piece, but provide the spark that makes the other colors work. So when matching yarns to the color sample, I always include those lesser colors to see what they do. As my design develops, I can add or remove colors, but it is often the seemingly less compatible colors, those that don't seem to go with the others, that raise the effect from the mundane to the exciting.

I will be forever grateful to Elizabeth Zimmermann, whose book, *Knitting Without Tears* (Scribner's, New York, 1971), profoundly changed my attitude towards knitting. What a wonder it was to read instructions that said to begin at the bottom—there would be lots of time to think about what to do at the top. Colorists can begin at the bottom, too; there is a world of opportunity waiting.

The important thing to remember is that no project is the ultimate; each is a step along the road. Enjoy, experiment, take chances, have fun: this is the learning process. Learning to see color, then using what we see is a lifetime project. I have yet to finish a piece that I couldn't visualize improvements to. I keep reminding myself of what a gallery-owner friend once told me. She said that she differentiates between art and craft, not by the medium, but by the attitude of the person who created the work. A craftperson produces the same thing over and over, an artist continues to change and grow. □

Dorothy Bird lives on a small island off the coast of Washington State. She is an artist who is best known for expressing her interest in color through knitting and weaving. Bird is the Curator of Crafts for the Janet Huston Gallery in LaConner, Washington. (Photos by Susan Kahn)

Stranding effortlessly— almost

by Alice Korach

Many people fear stranded knitting because they're sure that they'll produce "seersucker." The trick to keeping your knitting flat and your tension even is remarkably simple: Don't let the stitches you've knit pile up near the tip of your right-hand needle. Just keep smoothing and spreading them out along the needle as you go. You can crowd the left-needle stitches as much as you like, without dropping them.

If you get into the habit of spreading the just-knit stitches to their correct gauge width, particularly as you carry the new color behind them to begin using it, your floats will be exactly the right length, neither long and sloppy, nor too tight; and your knit fabric will be perfectly flat.

Classic stranded knitting requires that you carry one strand in each hand. Like any technique, this takes some getting used to. It was easy for me to learn the classic two-hands method because, as a child, I learned to knit throwing the yarn with my right hand. When I was a college freshman—knitting my way through lectures—I was introduced to Continental knitting, where the yarn is carried in the left hand and scooped into position by the right needle, with perhaps a small assist from the left index finger.

I always put the background color in my left hand, my preferred knitting method, and the pattern color in my right, since it's generally used a little less. This way, when I'm reading a chart as I knit, I automatically throw all the pattern stitches with the yarn in my right hand.

I recommend that you learn to knit with the method that you don't normally use: English/American if you knit Continental, or Continental if you knit English/American. It shouldn't take you more than a few hours of feeling awkward, which is a small price to pay for a very rewarding and quick technique— two-hand stranded knitting. □

Alice Korach is an associate editor of Threads.

Color Blending

Knitting with several yarns at a time offers opportunities for subtle shading

by Gillian Bull

because I don't dye my own yarns, I used to feel limited by the colors that were available from yarn companies. Wanting to incorporate subtle color shading into my garments, I discovered that knitting with two or more strands of fine yarn held together allows me to change one strand at a time and get intermediate, blended shades. Used by weavers and needleworkers to create new colors, this concept of color blending allows me to stretch a decent selection of commercial colors into a wonderful range of hundreds of shades.

I knitted the sweater shown on the facing page on a knitting machine with two strands of size 20/2 yarn. Knitting by hand with several strands of 20/2 yarn or two strands of 8/2 yarn (approximately worsted weight) gives a similar effect. The color blending, which results in subtly shaded horizontal stripes, can occur in the background, as I've done on the facing page, with a single color for the foreground design. Or you can use a solid-color background, and work color blending in the lattice design, for a totally different effect (see the lower photo on p. 14). Or knit a less-structured design and color-blend in both areas as I've done in the background photo at right.

Knitting a lattice design with color blending is as easy as knitting a two-color pattern (see *Basics, Threads* No. 46, p. 16). The only difference is that every few rows, at the end of a row, you drop one color and replace it with another. Following the diagrams and measurements on p. 15, you can use any fine yarns to knit the sweater on the facing page by hand or machine, working out your stitch and row gauge from a sample swatch.

Selecting yarns and colors

I often knit with one strand of wool and one strand of cotton yarn held together. I like the combination of soft wool and harder cotton textures, and they offer a wide range of color possibilities.

Maine Line wool yarn by JaggerSpun, one of my favorites, is available in sizes 20/2 and 8/2 from Halcyon Yarns (12 School St., Bath, ME 04530; 207-442-7909; 800-341-0282). They also sell 20/2 mercerized cotton and 8/2 Holmstead (unmercerized) cotton yarns. Both the wool and cotton yarns come on approximately 2-oz. mini-cones, a handy size for a sweater that includes many colors. For the solid color foreground, I often use a wool/rayon yarn such as Velveen, from Sunray Yarn (347 Grand St., New York, NY 10002; 212-475-9655).

To choose colors for a sweater such as the one on the facing page, I place a foreground color on the floor. Then I surround it with other colors, one at a time, until the combination excites me. Next, I arrange the colors in a circle around the main color, shading from dark to light, as they will appear in the sweater. Knitting small swatches with color blending, like those shown on the bottom of p. 14, tells me how the colors work together, and give me a preview of the completed sweater.

Working with color

There are many ways to combine yarns for blending. One of my favorite methods creates new shades by changing the strands one at a time, giving extra shades between the main colors. Take four colors of wool, for example, a red, brown, orange, and yellow, and four colors of cotton in a slightly different red, brown, orange and yellow. When you knit a swatch

From *Threads* magazine (April 1993) 46:42-45

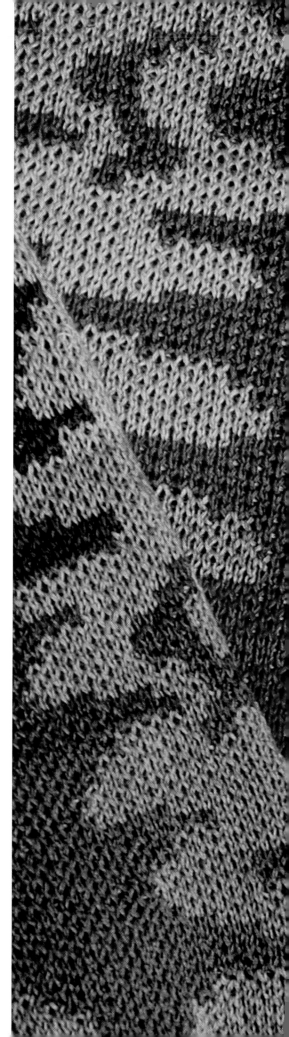

Photo by Yvonne Taylor

Knitting with two strands of yarn at a time and changing one strand every few rows yields subtle shading in the background of the sweater above while the foreground design remains a solid color. In the background photo, color blending occurs in the back- and foreground.

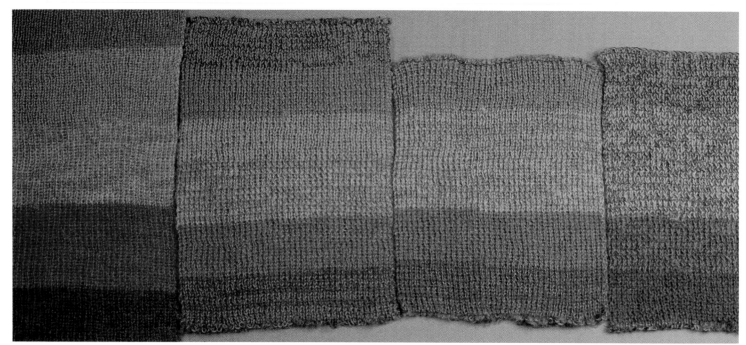

You can achieve a subtle form of color blending by changing one strand of yarn (the wool) and keeping the second strand (the cotton) constant throughout. From left to right: five colors of wool yarn knitted alone; then the same five colors blended with one strand of rust cotton, one strand of medium gray cotton, and at right, one strand of black cotton.

to experiment with this effect, use any shades that you like and have on hand. Knit several rows with one end of red wool and one end of red cotton held together; cut the end of red wool and tie on the brown wool. Knit the same number of rows with brown wool and red cotton. Cut the red cotton, and tie on the brown cotton. Now you have one end of brown wool and one of brown cotton; knit the same number of rows before cutting the brown wool and adding the next one, the orange wool. Keep knitting and changing

a strand at a time until you've worked through all the colors of wool and cotton.

A second way that I color-blend is to use one shade of cotton throughout, and just change the wool colors. The cotton evens out the colors of the wool. If I knit a muted cotton color, such as medium gray, with each main color, the whole look will be subdued. If I use a black or very dark color, the wool colors will sing. For examples, see the photo above. It never ceases to amaze me that one thread can make such a difference in the overall effect.

When you're ready to incorporate a swatched technique into a garment, you have to decide how many rows to knit with each color combination, which depends on the effect you want. You can change colors randomly, repeat the entire series of colors more than once, or shade the garment from dark at the bottom to light at the top (usually more flattering than the reverse), or from muted to bright.

To repeat each color combination evenly, divide the number of rows in the garment by the number of color combinations you're going to use. For example, if there are 384 rows in the body of the garment and 8 different combinations, you will knit 48 rows per color. Or you might decide to knit a certain number of rows of each combination regardless of the color changes, and see what happens.

As you work with color blending, many more ways to combine the yarns will occur to you spontaneously, each with a different effect. My color changes are more intuitive than mathematical; my mood and the weather play a big part in my decisions. Out of my studio window I can see Puget Sound, and the constant color changes on the water and the mountains often affect my color choices. But sometimes I need a break from color and enjoy the austerity of working on a series in black and white for a while. ☐

The same color blending looks very different when it occurs in the background, as in the swatch at left, and in the foreground, at right. A simple lattice design provides the pattern.

Gillian Bull designs knitwear on Bainbridge Island, WA, and markets her work under the label Diana Gillian Knits.

Making a color-blended sweater

Most knitters prefer to follow a written pattern using the prescribed yarn, but it's almost as easy—and much more fun—to knit a garment from a simple diagram. By following the measurements on the drawings below, you can knit the sweater shown on p. 13 in size medium by hand or machine.

If you're knitting by hand, experiment with size 8 needles using two strands of 8/2 yarn (one of wool and one of cotton), for about the same gauge as a worsted-weight yarn (4-5 sts/in.). Or, if you want a lighter-weight sweater with more subtle color blendings, try three strands of 20/2 yarn.

Knit at least a 4-in.-square gauge swatch for each stitch pattern to determine the number of stitches per inch (horizontal) and the number of rows per inch (vertical). Now you can figure out how many stitches and rows to knit for each garment section. Multiply the appropriate numbers (sts/in. for width, rows/in. for length) by the measurements below, beginning with the back (the easiest), to learn how many stitches to cast on (sts/in. X 23 in.) and how many rows to knit (rows/in. X 20 in.). Write these numbers next to the measurements on the diagram.

For the fronts, you'll determine how many rows to knit straight before decreasing 4 in. to shape the V-neck. Spread the decreases evenly over the 14-in.-long V. To space the sleeve increases evenly, subtract the number of stitches in the cuff from the number of stitches at the upper sleeve; divide ½ this total into the number of rows above the cuff. This gives the number of rows to knit between an increase at each edge.

Options for knitting motifs

As a former weaver, I borrow the pattern motifs for many of my sweaters from weaving designs. You don't need to be a weaver to use this idea in your knitting. Just take a piece of fabric with a strong woven pattern and copy the pattern motif onto graph paper, then knit from the graph paper, or punch it onto your knitting machine pattern card.

The two patterns in the sweater on p. 13, one in the body and one in the sleeves, are eight harness twill weave structures (see the body motif chart below left). They work well together because the open spaces balance each other.

For hand knitters, begin the body with 3 in. of ribbing or a checkerboard pattern. Then knit the body motif as a two-color Fair Isle, following the chart below. Using my first method of color blending (described in "Working with color" on p. 12), change the color of one strand every *x* number of rows. (This number will depend on how many shades you use and how many rows in the sweater section, according to your gauge.) Try a different woven motif for the sleeves, if you wish, or use the body motif throughout. For a buttonhole band, I sew a knitted cord to the garment edge, leaving openings where I want the buttonholes to be. You might choose to add a couple of rows of single crochet on each edge instead, for the button band and buttonholes.

Constructing the collar

The soft collar on this sweater looks complicated, but it's actually a simple rectangular piece of knitting sewn to the V-shaped neckline along one long side. By hand or machine, knit with a nonrolling stitch that looks good on both sides, such as garter, moss, or seed stitch (by hand) or double-bed jacquard (by machine). If your sweater's measurements are different from those drawn below, knit the collar the length of the two front V's plus the back-neck width. Measure after you've sewn the garment together, then knit the collar to complete the sweater. A button loop on the loose corner of the collar fastens it to a button on the body of the sweater.—G.B.

Pattern diagram for a medium-sized sweater

With the numbers you learn from measuring your gauge swatch (how many sts/in. and rows/in.), you can multiply by the measurements below to figure out how many stitches to cast on and how many rows to knit for each section.

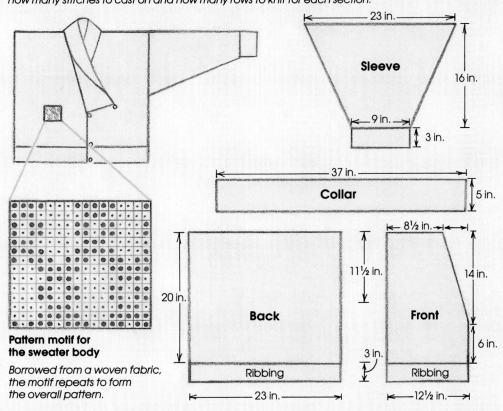

Pattern motif for the sweater body

Borrowed from a woven fabric, the motif repeats to form the overall pattern.

The attractive draped collar above, shown folded and fastened with a button and loop on p. 13, is a simple knitted rectangle that you sew along one long side to the V-shaped neckline of the sweater.

Impressionistic Knitting

Luxuriate in fine fibers and delicate details

by Arlene Mintzer

*i*once ran into an old friend whom I hadn't seen in a number of years. She asked me if I was still knitting. It was like being asked if I was still breathing.

I am a passionate yarn collector and have been for many years. I'd give up buying many things, but never a wonderful skein of yarn. It's almost always the yarn that inspires a piece for me. Over the past 15 years, I collected many of the yarns that I used for the vests in the photo at right. Some of them have special significance for me. I love color and am motivated by many different sources. I don't plan my color schemes. I collect all the potential yarns and add and delete colors as I see fit, letting the yarn inspire the knitting. I'm also inspired by antique Persian carpets, historic needlework samplers, Peruvian textiles, and paintings. One spring, I collected some fallen sycamore bark. The color range of sycamore bark is unbelievable—from familiar camouflage to beautiful grayish pinks, tans, lavenders, and rosy browns that are very subtle and extremely rich.

During the past four years or so, my inspiration has also come from my natural surroundings. I walk a great deal both for my mental and physical well-being. I don't always walk at the same time each day, so I can view the same surroundings bathed in different light. I particularly like to walk in a misty rain, when the colors of the trees and flowers are brilliant and totally inspiring.

But the major source of inspiration for the two pieces in this article is Vivaldi's "The Four Seasons." This concerto is filled with some of the richest colors and textures I've ever had the pleasure of listening to. I wanted to create fabrics that were as impressionistic in feeling, with colors and textures that were as harmonious and evocative of the changing seasons.

Yarns

Yarn is a very complex material. It can be smooth, hairy, shiny, dull, variegated, looped, slubbed, thick or thin, depending on its source and fabrication. A wide variety of wonderful fibers can be used in one piece with infinite design and color possibilities. The rich fabric of these vests is made of angora, mohair, cotton, silk, wool, and alpaca (see "Sources," p. 19). Each of these fibers has special characteristics and qualities that I wanted for the finished pieces.

Angora rabbits aren't killed for their fiber, the removal of which is beneficial to them. I used commercially spun angora, which is generally available in natural white or dyed colors, in the "Spring" piece and handspun, natural-colored angora in "Fall." Handspun angora is one of the most sensuous of all yarns. Many of the natural colors echo the soft gray-browns and fawns of the earth in fall and winter. The angora I generally use is very long and furlike. It's wonderful for creating soft shadows and a feeling of cold days with just a hint of snow in the air. I also use it to tone down areas where the colors are a bit too bright.

Mohair comes from the Angora goat. Goat fleeces are sheared much like sheep fleeces. Mohair is extremely lustrous, dyes well, and is excellent for creating a haze or glaze

Working with a wealth of fine yarns, varied stitch patterns, and even gemstones (yoke, upper left), Arlene Mintzer uses color and texture to depict her impressions of "Spring" (right) and "Fall" (left). "Spring" incorporates many of her favorite techniques. Plaited ribbing (armholes) retains its shape especially well, and seed-stitch popcorns are even more exciting when they're different sizes. Originally a crocheter, Mintzer finds that single crochets in the front and back loops of the collar bind-off make a solid, decorative edge. (Photo by Susan Kahn)

Schematic of "Spring" vest

Work collar out from neck edge, using three different sizes of needles and slight increasing to shape it.

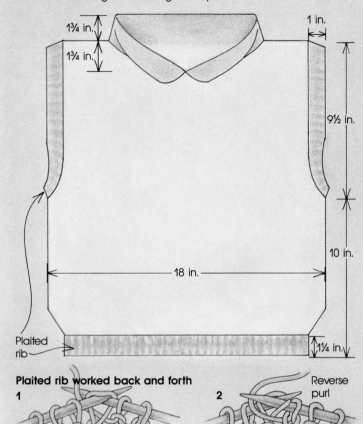

18 in. — 9½ in. — 10 in. — 1 in. — 1¾ in. — 1¾ in. — 1¼ in.

Plaited rib

Plaited rib worked back and forth

1   2   Reverse purl

Work knit stitches in normal manner, but work purl stitches from back, and throw yarn from under needle on all rows.

Plaited rib worked in the round

Work odd-numbered rounds reverse: knitting and purling in back of stitch and throwing yarn, as shown in drawings 2 and 3. Even-numbered rounds are worked normally.

3   Reverse knit

Interlaced running stitch

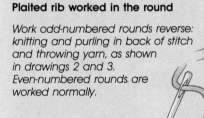

On seed-stitch fabric treat purl bumps as a row of running stitches. With a tapestry needle and contrasting yarn, lace loosely through bumps. Repeat lacing in other direction.

Illustration by Phoebe Gaughan

Special techniques

Plaited ribbing

Plaited ribbing is texturally exciting and retains its shape. To start, work a foundation row in plain k1, p1 rib. Begin the pattern on the second row.

Work *plaited rib back and forth* (multiple of 2 sts):
Row 1: *K1 (stitch won't cross until next row). Reverse p1: Insert needle from back to front and throw yarn under needle (drawing 2)*.
Row 2: Work as row 1. Stitches will feel tight as you work them and will twist. Repeat these two rows.

Work *plaited rib in the round* (multiple of 2 sts):
Rnd 1: *Reverse k1: insert needle through back of stitch and throw yarn over needle (drawing 3); reverse p1 (drawing 2)*.
Rnd 2: *K1, p1*. Stitches will feel tight as you work them, as you twisted them on rnd 1. Repeat these two rounds.

Popcorn variations

Seed-Stitch Popcorn 1:
This is a more voluptuous popcorn than a garter- or stockinette-stitch version. I start these on the fabric's right side and vary the size of the popcorns, even when I work them on the same row.
Step 1: *Purl into front of desired stitch, knit into back of it*. Repeat from *-* until you've worked desired number of stitches; end with purl. I usually work 5 or 7 sts for a fairly full popcorn.
Step 2: Turn work. Work p1, k1 seed stitch over popcorn stitches for as many rows as desired, turning after each popcorn row, usually 4 or 5 rows.

Step 3: With RHN, lift each popcorn stitch on LHN over first stitch, 1 st at a time, until only first stitch remains.

Seed Stitch Popcorn 2:
Step 1: Starting on wrong side of fabric, *p1, yo* into desired stitch three times, end p1.
Step 2: Turn. Purl across popcorn stitches.
Step 3: Turn. Work p1, k1 seed stitch across popcorn.
Step 4: Turn. Repeat Step 3.
Step 5: Turn. Sl3 k-wise, p2tog, p3sso (1 st at a time), p2tog, pass previously worked stitch over this one. 1 st remains.

Embroidery

Embroidery enhances a knit fabric and lets you change the fabric without ripping. I embellished a seed-stitch area of "Spring" by using the purl bumps as a base for *Interlaced running stitch* and adding French knots to the center of each circular motif formed by the running stitch.

Single-crochet collar edging

Work edging with right side of garment facing you.
Row 1: Work a sc in front loop (flp) of each bound-off collar stitch.
Row 2: Work a sc in back loop (blp) of each bound-off collar stitch.
Rnd 1: Work a sc in flp of each sc of row 1 and along narrow front edges of collar.
Rnd 2: Work a sc in blp of each sc of rnd 1, including narrow front edges of collar.
Next row: Work a slip stitch in flp of each sc of rnd 1, excluding narrow front edges of collar. —A.M.

---

over the fabric. The fibers catch the light in a very special way and add a halolike effect.

The *cotton* used in both pieces is mostly 6-strand embroidery floss. It comes in hundreds of lustrous colors, including variegated shades. I used a pastel mixture in "Spring" for the "berries" in the yoke section. Variegated floss is also wonderful for creating movement in a piece, especially

when worked in seed stitch. Dots of color created by the purl stitches seem to float past each other. The embroidery floss contributes the opalescence of nature's palette in all the vests.

Silk fibers of varying types result from different methods of processing the silkworm cocoon. I used a highly lustrous silk sparingly, as it would have been very ex-

pensive to buy many colors. Like the cotton, it adds a jewellike quality to the vests.

Wool has a diverse palette, which I love, and its elastic properties are especially important in these pieces—particularly in the ribbings.

Alpacas are regal looking animals with lovely, soulful eyes. Alpaca fiber comes in a vast array of natural colors and dyes beautifully to a lighter, more subtle tone than wool. The many natural gray-browns and beiges echo nature's hibernation in the "Fall" and "Winter" pieces.

Construction techniques

I generally start knitting at the bottom of a garment and work up. My interest isn't in complicated shaping techniques. I want to concentrate on the fabric itself, so I use classic shapes that fit well (see schematic, facing page). The back and front of the garment are constructed the same way, but the fabrics are totally different. Before I start, I work a large swatch, 6 in. wide by 4 in. long, in k1, p1 seed stitch, but that's the only pattern I swatch.

I worked all of these garments with needle sizes 0 through 2 and predominantly fingering-weight yarns. My gauge was about 8 sts to 1 in. There are, however, a number of angora and mohair yarns in the "Fall" and "Winter" pieces that were closer to a worsted-weight gauge of about 5 sts to 1 in. I've found that if you work no more than two consecutive rows with one of those yarns, the shape of the fabric won't become distorted. I also generally work the rows with heavier yarns somewhat tighter. I didn't find it necessary to change needle sizes. But if you want the fabric to pleat a bit, work the heavier yarn for several more rows.

All the garments have ribbed waistbands. One of them, "Spring," is plaited. Plaited ribbing, which I've recently discovered, has one of the most beautiful textures I've ever seen, as well as a great deal of elasticity (see photo on p. 17 and directions on the facing page). Making plaited ribbings is very time-consuming but well worth the effort. I always start my ribbings with wool and continue to work with it for several rows because it holds its shape very well. I used the same ribbing on the armbands, working short-row shaping at the lower edge of the arm-bands to taper them for a better fit.

For the body of these garments I used many different seed-stitch and slip-stitch pattern combinations, with popcorn accents throughout the yoke sections (see photo, p. 17). Seed stitch is wonderful for creating light and shadow in a piece because of the alternating smooth and bumpy knit and purl surfaces. It's ideal for use with varie-gated yarns since it breaks up the color, creating a pointillistic effect.

Slip-stitch patterns add visual excitement, highlighting certain yarns or colors. They're somewhat elongated and can therefore be made to either stand out or recede, depending on whether the thread is held behind or in front of the stitch being slipped.

Popcorn stitches are real favorites of mine. The berries that I worked into the yoke of the "Spring" piece needed the special tex-tural quality that only popcorn stitches could give them. I've experimented with numerous types of popcorns (two are described under "Special techniques," facing page, and can be seen in the photo on p. 17).

I play with my stitch patterns as I go. It isn't advisable to work more than about ½ in. in any one pattern, and sometimes the beginnings and endings of rows aren't identical, because my stitch-pattern multiples may not come out even. In a project like this, where front and back are different, this isn't a problem. You can even change patterns in the middle of the row or do some spontaneous Fair Isle knitting.

Although I generally work with a single yarn on each row, I sometimes combine yarns that are exceedingly thin to make one slightly heavier yarn. I'll combine, for example, a very fine weight wool with a strand of embroidery floss. These needn't be the same color. I change colors and yarns often, sometimes more than once in a row. I seldom knit more than two or three rows in one yarn or color. I always tie my new threads around the old ones with a single knot. I make sure to slide the knot as close to the base of the stitch as possible. Braids also help to hold the knots secured. These knots are not bulky, and they add structural stability to the garment. The fabric is also much easier to handle if the ends are knotted while the work is in progress.

One of the best lessons I've learned is never to rip out a row immediately after working it. Should you feel somewhat negative about its relationship to the rest of the piece, think about working with another color on the next row. This can mute or intensify the color of the questionable row, enabling you to tie it together with the fabric. Also, step back and look at the piece from a distance to see how the colors relate to each other. If you're still unsure about the color in question, try yet another row or two—you might be pleasantly surprised. You can also change the fabric by embroidering on top of it, as I did in the "Spring" piece (see the embroidery directions on the facing page).

Finishing techniques

Special finishing touches greatly enhance a piece for me. I hate to weave in ends—and it would be unbearably tedious with so many—so I braid them in three-strand braids. Every time I change yarns, I make sure that I leave ends at least 4 in. long for subsequent braiding—except at the very bottom of the piece, where they would hang out unattractively. I weave these ends into the seam without braiding them. But you could tack down the braid on the wrong side should braiding mania have overwhelmed you. Sometimes I even leave the braids on the right side for decorative purposes. I prefer to braid the ends before sewing the pieces together.

Although I knit much more than I crochet, I find that crochet is a wonderful medium for providing just the right finishing touch. It was the perfect accent for the collar edging on the "Spring" piece (see the crochet directions on the facing page).

Finally, I got a great deal of creative pleasure from sewing coral branches and turquoise tube beads to the centers of my popcorn details in the "Fall" piece. Just a few of these gemstones can really make the completed piece sparkle. I stitched them on with a No. 10 beading needle and fine, strong nylon thread. The stones can be hand-washed or dry-cleaned. I've also used fresh-water pearls, amethysts, and other naturally colored stones. Dyed varieties don't launder well and are especially sensitive to dry cleaning, so I don't use them.

For me, these pieces represent a very strong connection with the natural world, in both the impressionistic fabrics and the materials used to create them. The fabric is continually evolving, with subtle color and pattern changes that provide never-ending surprises for the viewer—much like the changing seasons. □

Arlene Mintzer teaches workshops nation-ally and is the owner of a mail-order business, The Sensuous Fiber, Box 44, Parkville Station, Brooklyn, NY 11204.

Sources

Retail
The Sensuous Fiber
Box 44
Parkville Station
Brooklyn, NY 11204
$2 for complete mail-order information; yarns, books, unusual tools for knitters and crocheters.

Wholesale
(Write or call for local distribution information.)
Kreinik Mfg. Co., Inc.
Box 1966
Parkersburg, WV 26102
(304) 422-8900
Au Ver a Soie silks.

Ironstone Yarns
Box 365
Uxbridge, MA 01569
(617) 278-5838
Mohair in heather shades.

DMC Corporation
107 Trumbull St.
Elizabeth, NJ 07206
(201) 351-4550
Cotton embroidery floss.

Plymouth Yarn Co.
500 Lafayette St.
Bristol, PA 19007
(215) 788-0459
Dyed and natural alpaca in fine weight.

One Small Stitch for Knitters

A giant step for color and texture

by Lynne Vogel

i have always been fascinated with color—its nuances, its illumination of form. I am continually amazed by the often impossible subtleties and impudent juxtapositions of color in natural objects: rocks, bark, fallen leaves. Today mauve, moss, puce, blue violet, and olive danced about me during a walk in the woods. I cannot just let this be. I must do something about it.

Knitted jackets, like the one shown opposite, are my canvasses for exploring color. When people first see the diamond-patterned fabric, they are often amazed that it was executed so easily. They believe I must have knit with two sets of needles, or embroidered or quilted over the knitting, or used some other equally time-consuming and complicated process. That could not be farther from the truth. I knit with an ordinary pair of straight needles and only one color per row. The stitch pattern, a simple combination of slipped stitches and long floats carried across the front of the work, can be quickly mastered with some practice to perfect the tension.

The trick to making a beautiful jacket is understanding how to make the floats stand out from the background by manipulating the yarn texture, and to blend the colors so they work together in the garment as a whole. With the jacket pattern and techniques on pp. 24-25, some trial and error, and a few color rules and the courage to break them, you're ready for exploration.

Glossy versus fuzzy

Stranded quilting, with soft puckers created by catching floats of smooth embroidery floss with stitches in a row of floss an inch above (see photo, right), is beautiful when rendered in two textures of the same color. Imagine downy white mohair crossed by diamonds of glossy white pearl cotton or fire-engine red mohair quilted with an equally vivid shiny red.

I use DMC No. 3 two-ply pearl cotton for the stranding because it does not stretch and fray as silk and rayon would. It is the shiniest cotton available, important for textural contrast. DMC No. 3 pearl is sold only in 16.4-yd. skeins, but it is reliably brilliant, colorfast, and easy to get at my local needlepoint shop (see "Sources" on p. 23 for mail-order information). ⇨

Author Lynne Vogel balances lustrous and fuzzy textures with dark and light colors for the perfect lightweight sweater. Try knitting your own version of the jacket at left with the pattern on pp. 24-25. (Photo by Yvonne Taylor)

Stranded quilting pattern

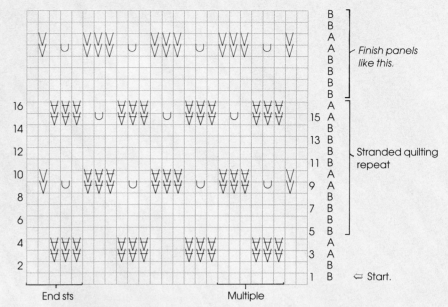

End sts — Multiple

- Finish panels like this.
- Stranded quilting repeat
- ⇦ Start.

Key to symbols

Note: Always slip as if to purl. Slip 1st st of every row for chain selvage.

 Sl 1 wyif (slip 1 st with yarn in front), RS.
Sl 1 wyib (slip 1 st with yarn in back), WS.

 Sl 1 wyib, RS.
Sl 1 wyif, WS.

 Knit under strands: Reach under floats of stranded rows below with right-hand needle as if to knit; insert needle into next st on left-hand needle; knit st; pull st under strands simultaneously (see photo below).

☒ **K2 tog.**

Step-by-step instructions

Corresponds with chart shown above.

Multiple of 6 sts, plus 1 st
(A) = pearl cotton.
(B) = mohair background.
Note: You can change background color every 2 rows, as desired.

Row 1 (RS)(B):
sl 1, knit.
Row 2 (WS)(B):
sl 1, purl.
Row 3 (A):
sl 1, k1, *sl 3 wyif, k3; rep from *, end sl 3 wyif, k2.
Row 4 (A):
sl 1, p1, * sl 3 wyib, p3; rep from *, end sl 3 wyib, p2.
Row 5 (B):
sl 1, knit.
Row 6 (B):
sl 1, purl.
Row 7 (B):
sl 1, knit.

Row 8 (B):
sl 1, purl.
Row 9 (A):
sl 2 wyib, *k1, U, k1, sl 3 wyif; rep from *, end k1, U, k1, sl 1 wyib, k1.
Row 10 (A):
sl 2 wyif, * p3, sl 3 wyib, rep from *, end p3, sl 1 wyif, p1.
Row 11 (B):
sl 1, knit.
Row 12 (B):
sl 1, purl.
Row 13 (B):
sl 1, knit.
Row 14 (B):
sl 1, purl.
Row 15 (A):
sl 1, k1, *sl 3 wyif, k1, U, k1; rep from *, end sl 3 wyif, k2.
Row 16 (A):
sl 1, p1, *sl 3 wyib, p3; rep from *, end sl 3 wyib, p2.
Row 17:
Repeat Rows 5-16 for pattern.

Catch the floats of pearl cotton with a knit pearl-cotton stitch five rows later.

The background yarns have a softer texture than pearl cotton. Mohair, handspuns, silk, rayon, wool, and blends, in weights from sport to worsted, are all appropriate choices. Brushed mohair is my favorite because of its light weight, soft hand, and loft. Keep at least half the background in brushed mohair so the garment will not be heavy.

The stranded quilting stitch

You can try out the stitch pattern (see the instructions and chart on p. 21) with a pair of size 8 needles and two colors of worsted-weight wool. All the slipped stitches and carrying of floats occur in the pearl cotton rows. To slip a stitch, just transfer it exactly the way it sits on the left needle to the right needle; for most people, this means to slip the right needle into the stitch on the left needle as if you were going to purl.

Whenever you slip a stitch, the yarn is carried past the stitch. The pattern calls for you to slip three stitches, holding the pearl cotton on the front of the work. The pearl cotton forms a float, a loose length of yarn. The float must be about 1 in. long so that when you catch it with a knit stitch to anchor it in the fabric several rows later, it won't severely pucker and distort the knitting.

Practice the stitch until you are satisfied with the tension of your stranding. The fabric will pucker a bit due to the juxtaposition of the slipped stitches and the floats that are caught by a stitch above. If your stranding is too tight, push each set of slipped stitches away from the needle tip as you are knitting to lengthen the floats.

After you've tried stranded quilting in one color, try changing the background color every two rows. To prevent floats along the selvage, twist the working yarn around the carried one at the beginning of every right-side row. You'll find that the fuzzy yarns soften the edges of the resulting stripes while shiny or smooth yarns serve to accentuate them. Manipulating color is the most obvious way to prevent the background from appearing too stripey, but the orchestration of texture is an indispensable tool for obtaining background harmony.

Color from around you

The actual process of working out a color way is inseparable from the experience that inspired that process in the first place. Invariably I find errors in my subjectivity, and the only way to discover and correct those errors is to reimmerse myself in the surroundings that first provided motivation.

Grouping your yarns by value, such as light or dark (top), guarantees a successful multicolor blend as indicated by the light, medium, and dark value sample swatches (bottom).

For instance, a recent combination of vivid blues, aquas, and olive greens just doesn't satisfy me. Why? I slow down and look at what surrounds me: ocean, sky, forest, and winter rains. Of course! I am trying to make the sky and ocean blue, yet during the rainy season the sky and sea are perpetually gray. When the surroundings are gray, blue looks colder than ever. I am trying to warm blue with olive, which actually looks a reddish brown next to the blue. Since olive is really a dark yellow, I laugh at myself. What is this blackened yellow, the midnight sun? How do I turn on the lights?

Tired of mulling over yarn, I bundle myself up and take the dogs out for a walk along the forested sea cliffs north of town. I see color combinations that I've been trying to work with all around me. Blue violet swathes the distant headland as aqua-gray waves dash against deep olivine sea rocks spotted with ochre and plum. Silvery green ferns, deep olive moss, and mauve lichens vivify the exquisite trunks of red-tipped alders, which are an indescribable soft red gray. The ferns, lichens, and moss seem to be the network that ties the rest of the scheme together.

Now reinspired, I rush home and pull out my mauves, puces, and moss greens to try a combination of subdued colors. I pull out muddy purples and some almost gray greens and work them into the pattern. The greens turn yellow again, and the mauves are not vibrant enough. As I sort through more yarn I come across two soft reds.

Thinking the reds are too bright, I toss them aside, but to my surprise they land with the gray blues. This is an unexplainable stroke of fortune because the haphazard toss actually provides me with the combination I would never have tried if I had obeyed my reason. I knit the soft reds with the gray blues, delighted.

Now I return to my vivid blues and aquas. Why not add a lively red? Since red and aqua are not quite complementary, they tend to enhance each other's brilliance without providing too much of a contrast.

Shade or hue

Ideally, the background of stranded quilting should gently undulate between luminous and shadowy. To achieve this without creating too much depth, you must avoid too many different types of contrast at once.

If you wish to use contrasting *hues* for variation—hue being intrinsic color like red, blue, or orange—especially when mixing warm and cool colors, you must keep all your hues at a similar *value*—the degree of light and dark. The yarns and swatches on the facing page will give you a concrete idea of the difference in brilliance that a change in value can make. It may surprise you to see that a dark value of yellow looks olive green or that light values of orange and violet both appear pinkish. If you limit the background to hues that are adjacent on the color wheel, you can use a wider range of values in the background.

When working in multiple colors, the pearl cotton should contrast somewhat in hue and value with every color in the background. Where the pearl exactly matches a mohair color, it will fade into the background, destroying the continuity of the two separate planes of color. The pearl contrast may be subtle, but it must be there.

I prefer to avoid using pure black, as it creates holes and deadens luminosity. A solid black is a dead black. Instead, try to achieve a black effect with hues at their darkest values.

Besides watching how you use contrast, keep an overall color effect in mind. This makes knitting more like painting because you must step back from your work periodically to keep perspective on the effect you are creating.

To achieve overall color balance, think about a unicycle rider. If she tips forward, she must lean backward to right herself. Pretend the wheel of the unicycle is a color wheel. As long as the wheel keeps turning, the rider will maintain her balance. Consequentially, the same color will come around again and again at regular intervals, sometimes faster, sometimes slower. As long as you have an overall color that you wish to achieve and you keep returning to that basic color again and again, you will find that you can successfully throw in some unexpected combinations. By experimenting, you will find that in learning to work within certain limitations, you will actually broaden your color language and you will be able to state your intentions far more accurately. ⇒

Lynne Vogel is a painter whose knitted work, under the name Milana, may be seen at Mobilia, 348 Huron Ave., Cambridge, MA 02138. Her jacket pattern follows on pp. 24-25.

Further reading

June Hemmons Hiatt, ***The Principles of Knitting.*** Simon & Schuster, Inc., 200 Old Tappan Rd., Old Tappan, NJ 07675; 1988; hardcover, $29.95.
Has some of the clearest illustrations I've seen in a knitting book.

Johannes Itten, ***The Art of Color.*** Van Nostrand Reinhold Company, 7625 Empire Dr., Florence, KY 41042; 1974; hardcover, $79.95.
My Dad, an animator, brought this book to my attention. Great for color theory, contrast, and design. The value chart on p. 55 relates 12 colors to a 12-value gray scale.

Barbara G. Walker, ***Charted Knitting Designs.*** Charles Scribner, dist. by MacMillan Distribution Center, attn: Order Dept., 100 Front St., Box 500, Riverside, NJ 08075; 1982; softcover, $19.95.
Wonderful for pattern ideas. Scale Quilting on p. 238 inspired my stranded quilting.

Sources

The Needlepoint
Shirley McCarthey, proprietor
123 S. Hemlock
Cannon Beach, OR 97110
(503) 436-0345
All DMC No. 3 pearl cotton. Sample card, $15, or will match your color sample.

Prism Yarns
Scandinavian Designs
607 East Cooper St.
Aspen, CO 81611
(303) 925-7299
Carries Prism mohair yarns, space dyed in five values; color cards, $5. Mohair cones in 15 colors; no cards, but explain to them what you need and they'll send samples.

Rio Grande Weavers Supply
Rachel Brown, owner
216B Pueblo Norte
Taos, NM 87571
(505) 758-0433

Offers 40 colors of custom-dyed mohair. Color cards for solids, and light and rich colors— $1.50 each. Will space-dye mohair (14 different "tweeds") with a min. order of eight 4-oz skeins; color card, $2.50.

Rowan Yarns
Distributed by Westminster Trading
5 Northern Blvd.
Amherst, NH 03031
(603) 886-5041
I recommend "Kaffe Fassett Kid Silk," a single-ply silk and kid mohair blend that comes in 13 colors. Write or call for a retailer near you.

Woolgatherings
Sandy Sitzman
HCR-61, Box 74-L
Banks, OR 97106
(503) 324-0701
Sandy custom dyes, cards, and blends six colors of handspun worsted-weight mohair/wool yarns. She will custom space-dye yarns in a requested color way. Color sample cards, $2.

A stranded-quilted jacket

When making a garment, I start with panels. Then, I can pick up selvages and knit in different directions, combining embellishment and assemblage. This creates visual excitement, saves finishing time, and, above all, fights boredom. These instructions are for making a jacket similar to that on p. 20.

Make small width adjustments by narrowing or widening connecting panels, rather than quilted panels. Stranded quilting must be worked in a multiple of 6 sts for the strands to be properly centered and positioned. Changing the quilted panel width means adding or subtracting in units of 6 sts or about 1 in. at a time.

The decrease method shown opposite maintains a border of 2 knit sts along the front neck edges, and avoids holes. Work a decrease at each edge for sleeves.

The first st of every row is slipped to create a chain selvage. This makes it possible to pick up sts along the selvage with the same size needle you use to knit, retaining your gauge without a lot of math.

I use cable cast-on (see *Basics, Threads* No. 37, p. 14) to start every panel. It's a sturdy, flat, non-stretchy edging that can be easily edged with crochet or picked up to begin another panel.

I use slip-stitch crochet (ssc) around the entire edge of every knit panel—just inside selvages and cast-on and cast-off rows—before picking up sts or grafting to another panel. Ssc just inside the single-crochet hem (see *Basics*) embellishes and fortifies it so it won't curl.

Instructions

This oversized jacket will fit sizes 10 to 14. You'll need about 240 yds. of DMC No. 3 pearl cotton—two boxes of skeins—and about 2 lbs. of mixed yarns. The gauge is about 6 sts/in. and 5 rows/in. using size 8 needles.

Back

1. Cast on 49 sts and knit panel 1 in stranded quilting pattern (see p. 21) for a total of 246 rows (25 in.). Bind off. Embellish entire bound-off edge just inside selvage with ssc (lower left drawing, facing page).
2. Knit panel 2 identical to panel 1.
3. Pick up selvage sts along the right side of panel 1. Knit 5 rows in a pleasing pattern. Try a fair isle pattern, with two colors in the same row, or a textured pattern such as a seed st or mosaic dot. Graft the last row of sts (left drawing below) to the selvage sts on the left side of panel 2.
4. Pick up bind-off and selvage sts along the top edge of the piece created from panels 1 and 2. Knit 1¼ in. in a pleasing pattern (panel 4). Bind off. Embellish edge with ssc.

Front

5. Cast on 49 sts and knit panel 5 in pattern up to about ⅓ the length of panel 1. Start shaping the neck edge at row 91. Dec 1 st every 6th row, as shown opposite, until 37 sts remain. Continue pattern to row 246. Bind off and embellish edges with ssc.
6. Knit and embellish panel 6 the mirror image of panel 5.
7. Pick up the bind-off sts along top of panel 5 and knit 2¼ in. in a pleasing pattern. Bind off. Embellish all edges of panel just inside the selvage with ssc.
8. Pick up sts along top of panel 6 and work as in step 7. Join fronts to back panel along bind-off sts.

Sleeves

9. Pick up selvage sts along entire right side of garment. Knit 1½ in. in a pleasing pattern (panel 9). Bind off loosely.
10. Pick up selvage sts along left side of garment and repeat as for step 9 (panel 10).
11. On the right side, mark center shoulder 2 to 3 rows forward of the front/back join. Pick up 91 sts along the bind-off for the sleeve, with st 46 at center shoulder; the same number of sts should remain in front and back side seams. Purl 1 row.

Begin stranded quilting pattern at pearl cotton rows (panel 11). Dec 1 st at each end of decrease row, using method shown for front-neck edges. Continue decreasing until 25% of sts remain on needle—23 sts. On next RS row: k3, k2tog across row; bind off. Without breaking yarn, ssc inside of bind-off sts on RS.

Pick up bind-off sts and knit cuff in a pleasing stitch.
12. Repeat for second sleeve.

Side seams

13. Graft together sleeve selvages (right drawing below) from armhole to cuff. Stitch jacket sides together with ssc, photo facing page.

Hem, double-layer collar, finishing

14. Pick up sts along bottom edge and knit 4 in. in a pleasing pattern. Bind off.
15. Pick up sts along front edges and neck. Knit stockinette for 3 in., purl 1 row RS for turn, and knit stockinette for 3 in. Fold band in half and sew in place on WS.
16. Single crochet (see *Basics*) along hem bind-off. Without breaking yarn, work back, embellishing single-crochet edge with ssc on WS.
17. Ssc the front collar edge through purl row of the fold in matching mohair, from the hem to the start of the V-neck angle.—*L. V.*

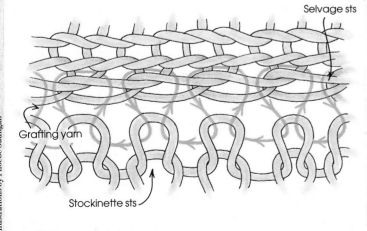

Grafting to a selvage

Selvage sts

Grafting yarn

Stockinette sts

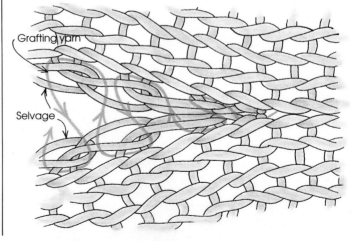

Grafting selvage to selvage

Grafting yarn

Selvage

Illustrations by Phoebe Gaughan

Schematic of Lynne Vogel's sweater jacket

Bold numbers for each section refer to numbered instructions at left.

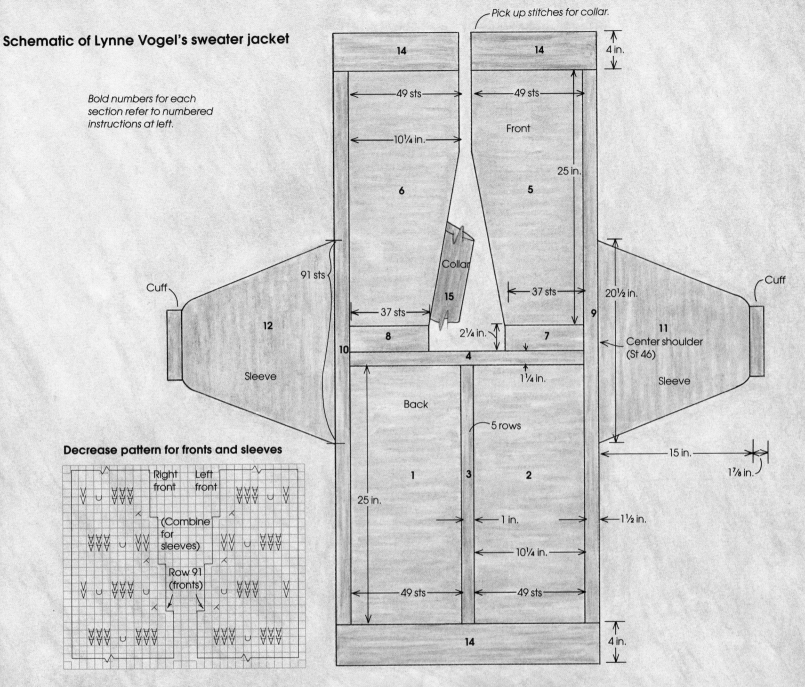

Pick up stitches for collar.

14 — 14 — 4 in.

49 sts — 49 sts

10¼ in.

Front

6 — 5

25 in.

Collar

15

37 sts — 37 sts

91 sts

20½ in.

Cuff — Cuff

12 — 9 — 11

8 — 7 — Center shoulder (St 46)

Sleeve — Sleeve

10 — 4 — 2¼ in.

1¼ in.

Back

5 rows

15 in.

1⅞ in.

1 — 3 — 2

1 in. — 1½ in.

25 in.

10¼ in.

49 sts — 49 sts

14 — 4 in.

Decrease pattern for fronts and sleeves

Right front — Left front

(Combine for sleeves)

Row 91 (fronts)

Slip-stitch crochet edging

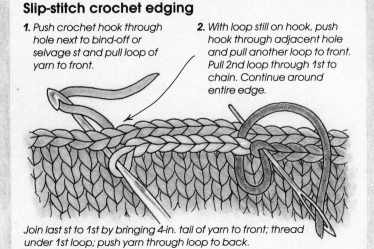

1. Push crochet hook through hole next to bind-off or selvage st and pull loop of yarn to front.

2. With loop still on hook, push hook through adjacent hole and pull another loop to front. Pull 2nd loop through 1st to chain. Continue around entire edge.

Join last st to 1st by bringing 4-in. tail of yarn to front; thread under 1st loop; push yarn through loop to back.

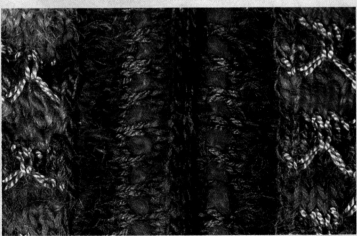

Side seam: Join the jacket front and back wrong sides together with slip-stitch crochet. The bind-off sts lie side by side, forming a decorative ridge (above).

From Graph to Garment

Knitting that's rich in color and texture starts with images from life

by Rosella Paletti

Simple textured stitches combined with color bring the images of the author's jacket to life. Moss-stitched red spirals stand out from the black background of Rosella Paletti's sweater "Lovesong for Pam and Cindy." (Photo by John Gilbert)

*i*t is very important to me that what I make touches the hearts of other people, and knitwear is a fantastic medium for this because it is out in the public arena of everyday life.

A *good idea* is most important. I use the events and experiences in my own life as my inspirational trigger: the birth of my child, the death of my friend, an illuminating moment in a tree fern forest. Personal experiences like these give me a strong and limitless reference point for visual images. Each idea gives me a repertoire of visual symbols to draw on.

My knitwear designs spring from a subconscious creative process. I start by discovering and putting onto paper images that are symbolic of my emotional response to the world around me. Then I draw a garment schematic and experiment with the placement of images and colors. The final schematic includes the charted designs and plans for areas of textured stitches. I use this method when designing a new line for limited commercial production, as shown on p. 28, or an exhibition piece, like the one on the facing page.

Design exercises

When you are starting out, use what is familiar to you as your idea or frame of reference. You may love plants, birds, or children. Anything can be a source of inspiration. For example, "Jacket for Jenny," detail above, was inspired by my home life—children, plants, cats, love, spirals (my personal symbol for thoughts and ideas), and eyes.

Write down any ideas in words. Think about your own visual symbols or language that represents your view or experience of life. Then make little sketches of your ideas that you can refer to later if you get stuck. Be adventurous! But most of all, put your heart into it. This is what makes something unique and gives pleasure to others as well as to yourself.

I sketch my ideas and symbols in a workbook or journal into which I also stick any pictures, photos,

Purl stitches in the background colors help to separate background and foreground elements in Paletti's 1988 cardigan "Jacket for Jenny." At upper right, you can also see how the lower part of a face extends onto the cuff ribbing. (Photo by Rosella Paletti)

or articles that relate to the idea I am focused on at that moment. For example, my experience of death has been: tears, love, mysticism, energy flowing inward and outward, humanity, children, seed pod, and new life, as shown in some of the sketches below. I also draw up a few rough sketches of the finished garment, experimenting with colors and shapes. If I get stuck at any point, I look back to the original idea for new inspiration and images.

Another idea is to cut out paper designs. For example, I recently made a series of black paper cutouts inspired by a day in a tree fern forest in Tasmania. I used a scalpel blade and heavy black paper to cut out the original design, much like making a stencil. Sketches for the finished jacket, "One Day in a Tree Fern Forest," were the next step. I experimented with different arrangements of the cutout motifs on a rough schematic shape. The last step was to draw up the final schematic with the gridded design and have the jacket knit. I also used my cutouts as the design for printed fabric, embroidered felted work, and printed paper. The pillow-top pattern on p. 29 is based on the same motifs and will give you a feel for how I work with gridded designs.

Getting the design on paper

By the time I sit down at the graph paper, I have a fairly accurate picture of what I plan to make, having developed my motifs and made a rough sketch of the garment.

Charting the garment—To draw up a schematic of the garment, I use 2mm, blue-green graph paper sheets (5 squares per cm), which makes a readable, to-scale graph of the garment that's usually compact enough to fit on a single sheet. I also use a sharp lead pencil and a right triangle ruler to make a to-scale outline of all the pieces. Initially, it's a good idea to use a plain commercial pattern to give you shaping and stitch count. When the schematic is completely accurate, I draw it in with a permanent ink pen. But since spontaneity is important to me, I often make changes as I knit, immediately penciling them in for future reference.

The shapes of my garments are simple, comfortable, and practical. As the focus in my work is on the picture, I use an uncomplicated, reliable pattern for the structure, as shown in the schematic for a typical short jacket on p. 28. You must get the math right. Knit a sample swatch of your idea first to check the gauge. For example, I work at 5½ stitches to the inch in eight-ply Australian DK (double knitting) wool (approximately a three-ply weight in U.S. sizing) on 10 and 8 English needles (U.S. sizes 3 and 5). Everyone knits differently, so you need to swatch carefully for your particular gauge in order to determine exact stitch counts and shaping directions.

Charting the images—Draw in the shape of your garment, according to the measurements, on a larger-grid graph paper so the knitting pattern will be easy to read. Then roughly draw in your visual image. Remember:
• Synchronize the shoulders, sleeves,

A short garment with set-in sleeves and pi-cot trim is becoming to many figures. Pal-etti's typical short jacket shape shown in the schematic at lower left combines limit-ed shaping with a variety of images from her personal symbols for a very sophisti-cated garment. (Photo by Susan Kahn)

fronts, and side seams so that the pattern flows.

• Don't change colors less than three stitches from the edges. You need one stitch for sewing up.

• Have a minimum of two stitches for any one color (unless you're doing Fair Isle or you particularly love sewing in ends—see *Threads* No. 40, p. 14 for information on finishing ends).

• Avoid garment patterns that increase/ decrease in the body of the garment. It is easier to keep shaping at the edges.

• Denote the center of any piece with a broken red line on the graph.

• Number the graph both horizontally and vertically in units of ten at the pattern's edge to help you keep your place.

• Increase/decrease symmetrically on both sides.

I almost always work with square-grid graph paper. My ability to make a mental translation from a square gridded design to the oblong shape of knitted stitches is the result of practice. Intarsia knitting with many colors and yarns tends to produce an almost square gauge, unlike stockinette knitting with a single color. But you still have to remember that you'll probably need to knit more rows than are drawn on your original sketch when transferring it to graph paper.

Avoid drawing into the band at the bottom of a garment; it's very tricky. I once did a person's face with a hand waving on the back of a vest. The wrist turned out too fat because I'd started it on a ribbed band, where the stitches were contracted, and then let it flow up into the stockinette body of the vest.

For particularly critical areas like a tonal detail of a face, I sometimes use knitters' graph paper in which the grid is a true knitted stitch proportion. I photocopy enlarge it because a bigger grid is easier to read while knitting.

Another way to get things in the right proportion is to draw your picture to size on an outline of the sweater piece on a sheet of plain white paper; use another garment, if necessary, to get the proportions. As you are knitting, measure your knitted piece against the drawn image, and you'll see how you may need to adjust your instructions, adding a row here and there to what you've charted. Be flexible. Leave yourself scope to change the

Short jacket schematic, medium size
(measurements in inches)

design. I also recommend that you get the feel for this by practicing on small pieces like the "One Day in a Tree Fern Forest" cushion pattern below right. If it makes you feel any better, for commercial production, I often have to have an idea knitted twice to iron out all the faults.

Working with color

Color is something to enjoy, not to be afraid of. Its use is purely a matter of personal taste. The more you experiment with it, the more you will know what you do and don't like. Take risks. Be adventurous. I don't believe in a lot of rules. But it's a good idea to draw a to-scale drawing front and back of your garment and color it in. Try different combinations of colors. It is easier to detect what you do and don't like through drawing before committing yourself to knitting. I use a lot of black, as it doesn't show the dirt, and also because it's dramatic and suitable for day or evening wear.

A simple and effective way to add exciting visual effects to your garment is by using many tones of one color. For example, if you denote an area "red," use several different shades of the same ply, from pink through red to orange. Change the wool randomly, as your mood takes you. The more frequent the change, the more interesting the effect.

A recent jacket was inspired by a series of drawings and a story by my child. As the figures were fairly simple, I decided on a multicolored background to give a more interesting and dramatic effect. I gave my knitter a big bag of different colored wools, which she used at her discretion for a controlled space-dyed effect.

Working with texture

I also encourage spontaneity in using simple texture stitches to build up the interest in an otherwise flat area or around plain figures to highlight them. By changing from knit stitch to purl stitch, moss stitch, or ribs, for example, you can add a great deal of interest without the hassle of changing colors—and all those ends. Isolated areas of simple texture have very little effect on the overall gauge. If you maintain the same level of spontaneity with the texture and color of each piece as the garment is knitted, you will achieve an overall uniform effect.

After a while, the knitters who work for me know what end product I am looking for in terms of surface texture, and they will suggest certain stitches that create that idea with a minimum of effort. This may be as simple as knitting all the red spirals in moss stitch to highlight them from a flat, black background, as we did in "Lovesong to Pam and Cindy," shown on p. 26. Different knitters are familiar and comfortable with different textured stitches. Slip your favorites into a flat area to produce interest and uniqueness without too much effort.

I also like embroidering on knitting, as shown in "Lovesong to Pam and Cindy," where I embroidered details on each little person and highlighted areas with small glass seed beads. I'll talk more about my embroidery techniques in an upcoming article. □

Rosella Paletti's limited-production garments are carried by Mobilia, 358 Huron Ave., Cambridge, MA 02138. Besides designing knitwear and printed textiles, she draws, paints, embroiders, prints, constructs, decoupages, beads, and teaches.

A gauge square that's also a pillow-top pattern

Rosella Paletti's papercut inspired by a visit to a tree fern forest became a sweater, printed fabric, and this pillow top. To knit a 12- to 13-in. square, you'll need a gauge of 5½ sts/in. The pillow at right was knit with 50g each of black and white Maratona by Lane Borgosesia on size 7 needles. This yarn and gauge produces nearly square knitting, so you probably won't have to add rows. If, however, you do need a few extra rows to knit the design square, place them as suits your taste. Judge squareness as you knit by paying close attention to the shape of the little figures. Also note that the center lines divide the cushion into four smaller squares. See Basics, Threads No. 41, for information on how to twist yarns at color changes.

You may want to add 1 to 2 extra stitches/rows at each edge for additional selvage when sewing the top to a fabric back. Steam or block the top after securing all ends. Rochelle Harper's instructions for making a pillow sham (Threads No. 41) offer finishing suggestions. —R.P.

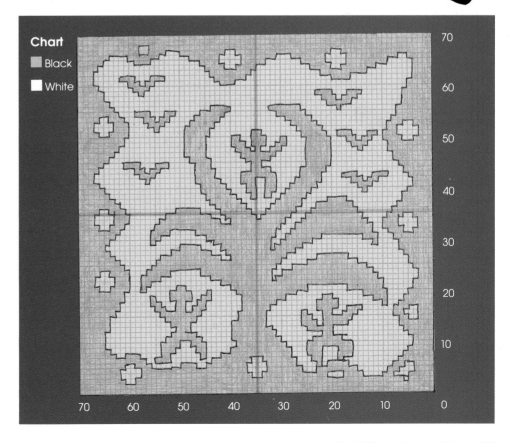

Chart
■ Black
□ White

You don't need to be an expert knitter to make a sweater that will turn heads. Inger Sandberg uses simple techniques and a basic shape and knits with a wild variety of colors and yarns as her mood and imagination direct. (Photo by Susan Kahn)

Letting Go of the Rules

Patternless knitting with yarns you have at hand

by Inger Sandberg

My mother never did anything with her hands. "Needlework is wasted womanpower." That was the message she gave me, and I believed her. Intellectual activities, music, and art became my interests.

In the '70s I started to suspect that my mother had been wrong. When my youngest son, Mathias, and I went to Tunisia for a week, I discovered The Yarn at the camel market where I bought two kinds—one very thin and one very thick. Mathias, the carrier, complained a lot about the funny seeds imbedded in the yarns, about the heat, and about the awful smell.

I wish I could show you what I did when I returned home to Sweden. I bought a simple pattern, just garter stitch, and a pair of large needles. When I finished the sweater, it looked funny. It was short but had ape-length sleeves. Dropped stitches made holes all over. And you won't believe it—I had sewn the sleeves together as the body and had made the front and back into sleeves! I started all over again with the thick yarn and *thin* needles. Now I enthusiastically knitted a small, itchy, hard-as-stone sweater. I could place it on the floor, and there it would stand by itself. After that, I decided to learn *how* to knit. I bought blue and white yarns at a sale, and I knitted lots of sweaters in different sizes from one pattern. Since I have a big family,

the sweaters always fitted someone. In a few months' time, the family looked like a football team in blue and white.

January 1979 was a turning point for me and my knitting. My husband, our son Mathias, and I completed a trip around the world to promote our books. Back home, I felt empty of words. An author who cannot write has to do something entirely different; so I took New Zealand yarns and started to knit my memories of all the wonderful places that I'd been.

Today knitting is two things for me: a new way of watching, and the technique. My knitting has taught me how to see. I strive to use yarn just the way I would use paint on a canvas. Yarn is soft, sensuous, and available in a multitude of rich, vivid colors and a variety of structures. It has a character of its own; yet it is pliable enough to accept the new horizons and applications I have for it. After my first landscape sweater, I began to look at nature in a more focused manner: the light in front of my eyes in the lake

where I swim or just before the thunderstorm; the clouds outside the airplane windows; the rocks and pebbles that my grandchildren and I take home from the creek; the braveness of the blueberry bushes that rise out of the clear-cut forest floor. Since an official trip my husband and I made to Venezuela in 1989 to attend the opening of the Swedish picturebook exhibition, my knitting palette has expanded to include startling colors that combine impressions and feelings and new subjects including faces, as shown in the photo on the facing page. ⇨

An initial disaster can lead to the dreaded disease "Knitter's Obsession," as Lasse Sandberg's cartoons (right) of his wife's knitting mania testify.

From *Threads* magazine (August 1991) 36:38-41

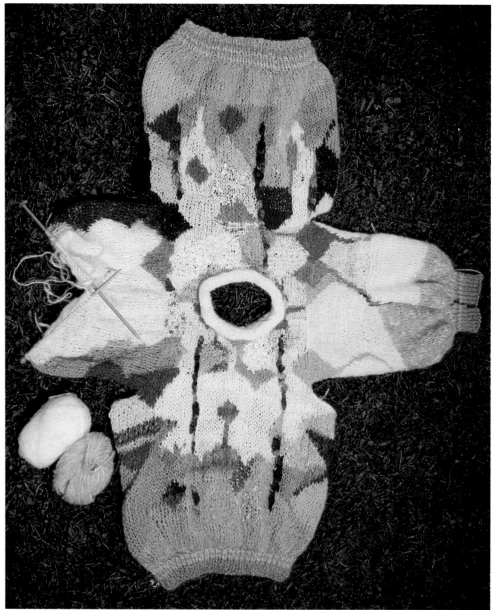

After knitting the front and back and joining the shoulders, Sandberg picks up between the bound-off armhole stitches and knits her sleeves straight to the cuff. (Photo by Lennart Edling)

Designing techniques

The techniques I favor make it possible to throw away the fear of not doing the right thing and to get rid of all the old rules of how to work with needles and yarns. I mix every kind of yarn in the same garment. I use Eisako Noro's cotton ribbon together with silk, mohair, angora, wool, metallic, viscose, acrylic, polyester—everything!

I keep my many yarns in boxes marked by color—green, blue, and so on. Before I start a sweater, I look in my boxes and think about what kind of sweater I want to make—landscape, season, mood, scenery, event, for example. In Sweden, where the winter makes our days so incredibly dark, I try to make the lightest, brightest, and most colorful sweaters during our dark months. Up here we need the vitamins that come through light and color. When I have

picked out the yarns I want to use, I sometimes make a drawing of my idea. Then I forget all about my plans as I knit along. I play a lot and enjoy myself all the time.

I only put my design on gridded paper when I need to have more control, like for a face. It is no fun if the nose ends up in the armpit. My method is very unsophisticated. I take four sheets of cross-ruled paper and tape them together to make it big enough. Every square represents a stitch, and I make a rough outline of the garment piece so I have an idea about where to begin and end.

All my sweaters are one-of-a-kind. I sometimes use the same theme two or three times, but since I knit from my inner vision everything changes. Backs and fronts are different from each other and so are the sleeves. I like the sweaters to be art-wear, in-

teresting to look at as the people wearing them move around; soft, moving sculptures. Most of the time, I make the same sweater shape. The variations come with the yarn, colors, and feelings.

When I started to knit, I often based my sizing and shaping on a conventional pattern that looked simple and that I thought would fit. Within that framework and size I played with my yarn and ideas. My ambition was to make sweaters big enough for people who love nice dinners. It is interesting to try my sweaters on people. The same one looks nice on my daughter-in-law who weighs less than 50 kilos (110 lb.) and my friend Mari-anne, who is more than 100 kg (220 lb.).

Knitting techniques

My sweaters are easy to make. I need a variety of yarns to choose from, in as many colors, weights, and textures as possible. Nowadays I use "traveling-needles" in different sizes. They have very short, metal points that are fixed to a plastic cord ending in a small plastic disc. The size of the needle is indicated on the end-disc, which also serves to stop the garment in process from sliding off. (Inox-Flex or Turbo Flex are two good brands.) I prefer these needles to circular needles, but both kinds are good when you work with heavy garments like mine.

In 1987 I discovered that I had come up with the same kind of technique as Kaffe Fassett, working with many short pieces and knitting in the ends while changing colors and yarns. When I also found out that I sometimes had done horizontally striped ribs like his, I changed so my stripes went vertically down through the ribs from the sleeve picture. I don't recommend it. It takes an awful lot of time.

When I start a sweater I usually start with the front or back ribbing, often using double yarns, and unless I'm using all wool, I knit in a thin elastic thread in matching colors throughout the entire ribbing. Since I use so many different yarns, some of which having no elasticity, this is very important, especially for the cuff. To prevent loops in the elastic, I stretch it as I knit. On the first row after the ribbing, I increase about 20 sts (4 or 5 in.) evenly. Then I change to larger needles. I use a half-size larger needle for my knitting than for my purling because I purl much looser than I knit. Frequently, I use double yarns up to the place where I bind off 12 sts (2 to 3 in.) on both sides for the armholes. After that, I knit the sweater straight up using smaller needles and one yarn instead of double yarns. Sometimes I make up to three needle changes as I approach the neck. This shapes the armscye/chest area enough that I don't have to do any fancy shaping, as you can see in the pictures at left and on p. 30. I try to shape the neckline in the simplest way. About 2 in. from the end, I bind off slightly fewer than one-third of the total stitches in the center. Then I decrease on either side of the bind-off until one-third of the total stitches remains on each shoulder. I want to be able to pick up about 100 sts (exactly how many depends on the thickness of the yarn) around the neck.

I join one shoulder seam by knitting the front to the back (see *Basics, Threads* No. 36) before I make the neckband. Then I pick up my hundred or so stitches and knit the collar in stockinette from the right side. I often use elastic in the first three or four rows, and sometimes, to make the collar larger, I change to a thicker needle after I've knit a few rows. It all depends on the yarn and on how I feel. When it's finished, it will form itself into a roll with the purl side out. Then I knit the other shoulder together.

Now it is time to begin the first sleeve. I always start by picking up stitches from the shoulder across the straight part of the arm-hole, as shown in the picture on the facing page. I knit a very wide, straight sleeve until I want to start the cuff. Then I reduce the amount of stitches over two rows to about 40 sts. Sometimes I make the ribbed cuffs very long. It depends on the style. When the cuff length is suitable, I bind off.

Finishing techniques

Before finally sewing a sweater together, I block it to shape. I lay it on a large, wet towel with a large checkerboard pattern that takes the place of a measuring tape, and I push thumbtacks right into my studio floor to hold the sweater until it dries. But if the sweater has a lot of acrylic or other man-made fibers, I just steam it to shape.

To make sure the sweater goes together right, it's important to sew the side of the sleeve to the armhole bind-off (12 sts) on the body back and front before sewing the side seams. Then I sew one long seam from cuff to bottom ribbing on each side. Finally, I sew the remaining collar seam together from the knit side.

I turn my sweaters inside out and hand-wash them with hair shampoo and cream rinse, especially if the majority of yarns are wool or mohair. After rinsing, I put the sweaters in a net bag and spin-dry them in the washing machine for about 45 seconds. They have to finish drying on a flat surface, and I shake them two or three times while they're drying. But I avoid washing as much as possible and air my sweaters outdoors between wearings.

When I wrote my knitting autobiography, *Mina glada tröjor (Happy Knitting)* (Kris-tianstads: Rabén & Sjögren, first ed. 1987, second ed. 1988), I wanted to encourage everyone who, like me, was a "failure" in needlework. Everything I have done is based upon trial and error, a slow but rewarding process. I also wanted to prevent people from falling into the same traps I had. And, of course, I also wanted to thank all the people who had come up to me on the streets and said, "You make me so happy! I love your sweater!"

I believe that we all need to be creative and artistically brave in what we are doing. We need to challenge the authority who states that there is just one way to do something. There are always ways to bend the rules. This will make the knitters happy, the yarn industry rich, and will reduce the tyranny of patterns. I'm certain that if I have been able to free-knit sweaters for the last 12 years, you can too. □

Inger Sandberg and her husband, Lasse, of Karlstad, Sweden, have together written and illustrated more than 80 children's books, which have received many awards and have been translated into 27 languages. They have also authored numerous television programs featuring their book characters.

Landscape sweaters like those on the line and those worn by Inger and Lasse Sandberg are fun and easy to knit without a pattern or plan. Inger Sandberg charts only when she knits representative images like "the little ghost Godfrey" at far left. (Photo by Lennart Edling)

A Subtle Patchwork Cardigan

Knitting and sewing make good use of leftover yarns

By Tamsen McAndrews

Sorting out a hamper full of leftover yarn one snowy November night, I was surprised by how many balls I had of each color. Seeing all the rich, subtle shades of red heaped together inspired me to combine them, and the concept of my patchwork cardigan was born.

A patchwork cardigan is not difficult to make, and it combines both knitting and sewing. Your personal design starts with a commercial sewing pattern or a knitting pattern diagram. When you divide the pattern into sections to knit, you determine how simple or complicated it will be.

Each section, which can be knit to shape or knit as a simple rectangle and cut to shape, can have a different texture or pattern. After assembling the sections with strips of a nonraveling fabric to form the main pattern pieces, you construct the garment using standard sewing techniques. The jacket can be soft, like a sweater, or more structured, depending on the style and interfacing you choose. Ribbing at the hems and front bands contributes to the sweater look, while fabric hems and facings give a sewn look. And a full lining adds polish.

Preparing the pattern

A simple pattern with minimal shaping and seams works best and is easy to divide into sections. You can begin with a sewing pattern for a basic jacket, such as Vogue 7752, McCall's 6434, or Burda 4328. If you're using a knitting schematic, you'll need to make a full-size paper pattern to help in measuring the sections and cutting the lining. Or you can design your own simple garment shape on graph paper and make a pattern (see the diagram for my red jacket on the facing page).

Patches of your favorite stitches knit with leftover yarns are assembled on the sewing machine for a versatile, fully lined jacket.

Photo by Susan Kahn

From *Threads* magazine (August 1993) 48:58-62

Designing a patchwork jacket

Here's how you'd draw on a commercial sewing pattern or a knitting diagram to design your own sweater. (The design shown is for the cardigan on the facing page). You can draw lines right on the pattern pieces to define sections to knit in each stitch pattern, using shapes that enhance your figure. Straight lines at armhole and neck make shaping easier. Every section is attached to the adjacent one with a strip of fake suede (see detail). Shorten pattern to make room for ribbing, if desired.

19 in.

Back

⑤ B ① C ② ④ A D ③ E

Rib

2 in.

15 in.

7 in.

10 in.

H ① I ② F G K J ⑥ ⑤ ④ ③

Front

32 in.

5 in.

Rib

Mark each section alphabetically. Note that left and right sides are the same, just reversed. Number the seams in order of assembly, beginning with short seams.

Knitted sections

½ in.

1-in. Ultrasuede strip

¼-in. seam allowances

24 in.

Sleeve

④ L M ③ ① ②

Rib

21 in.

2 in.

In detail: Every section can be knit or cut to the exact dimension outlined on the pattern since the section edges butt together.

Pattern proportions—Before dividing the pattern pieces into sections, you'll need to fit the pattern and adjust its proportions. If you decide to finish the lower edges of the body and sleeves with ribbing, shorten the length of the pattern pieces accordingly.

Seam allowances—One time-saving aspect of the jacket design is that, for the most part, you don't need to add seam allowances. The edges of the knit sections butt one another and the fabric strip holds them together, so the basic pattern dimensions remain the same, as shown in the drawing above. If you're using a sewing pattern, trim away the seam allowances on the pattern pieces where there will be fabric strips, such as at side seams, shoulders, and straight armholes.

For seams that will not be finished with fabric strips, such as a curved armhole and

sleeve cap, you do need a seam allowance. If you decide to use fabric facings for a more constructed jacket, leave the seam allowance at the neckline and center front.

Dividing the pattern into sections

Since you need no seam allowances for the knit sections, it's easy to draw the sections right on the pattern. I usually design the left and right sides of the jacket as mirror images, to balance the garment. Sketch small versions of the jacket on paper to experiment with a few ideas and options before drawing on the pattern itself.

I recommend that you use straight lines in your design, for several reasons: Straight fabric strips support the knitted sections, and it's difficult to sew fabric strips smoothly around curves, which tend to bubble in the finished jacket. As you draw, keep in mind

that the size and shape of the sections determine the overall effect of the jacket, and you can draw them to enhance your body shape. For example, a V-shaped section from the shoulders to the waistline will broaden the look of your shoulders and narrow the waist. And long, slim sections from the shoulders to the bottom will give the appearance of additional height. See my layout for ideas above.

I start by designing the back, because it's the largest uninterrupted space and suggests the overall design for the jacket. The front and sleeves come next. I often like to match the front and back sections at the shoulder.

And don't forget pockets. I prefer in-seam pockets made from lining fabric. They can be hidden in the side seams or between sections that fall vertically or horizontally in the pocket area. Use a sewing pat-

tern to determine their size, shape, and location. Or you can add knit or suede patch pockets, stitched between vertical strips of fabric. You would first line the pockets, then layer the patch pocket over the knitted section, and treat the two layers as one when adding the fabric strips.

After you're happy with the design in the small sketches, use a ruler to draw the sections on the pattern pieces. Label each section of the garment alphabetically for later reference. Your pattern pieces will be the map you use to complete the entire jacket, so make sure you're satisfied with the design before you start knitting.

Selecting yarns

My most successful patchwork garments contain yarns that have subtle color variations. Combining many different colors in a jacket can create a choppy look and destroy the

The varied textures and subtle shades of yarn are unified by strips of luxurious faux suede which join the knitted sections together and provide additional support.

lengths and weights vary tremendously; an advantage to using leftover yarn is that your previous garment will help you calculate how much area the yarn will cover.

Choosing stitches

When you're ready to select stitches for the jacket sections, let your imagination roll. Comb through your knitting books and think of every favorite stitch you've ever used, then pick a place for it in your jacket. You can use a cable down the outside of the sleeves, a V pattern up the center back, a seed-stitched shoulder, or a bubble-stitched front. Avoid openwork patterns in areas that will be interfaced, such as shoulders, necklines, and front edges, because the interfacing will show through the holes.

You need not use decorative stitches for all of the sections. Some nubby or fuzzy yarns provide plenty of texture when knitted in a garter or stockinette stitch.

Two knitting methods

You can begin knitting with just a general idea of the yarns and stitches you would like to use, and change your mind as you work on the jacket. I find it helps, however, to list each section by letter (as marked on the pattern; see the drawing on p. 35) in a notebook next to the yarn and quantity, planned stitch, and needle size or knitting-machine setting. Armed with this information, you are ready to start knitting.

Knitting to shape—Because the sections are small, you don't have to worry about the accuracy of the gauge the way you would for a large piece of knitting. A small error in the gauge produces only a small variation in the size of the section. I don't like to spend a lot of time knitting a gauge swatch for each section. Instead, I estimate gauge by using or combining the following methods: Refer to the yarn label for the recommend-

ed needle size and gauge; check the gauge from a pattern that uses the same yarn; rely on your experience with a similar type and weight of yarn; and, finally, cast on an estimated number of stitches for the section width, spread them out and measure, then add or subtract stitches to reach the desired width.

It's better to knit a section slightly smaller than the pattern size, rather than larger. If you stretch a section to shape during blocking, it will retain the new shape, because of the tension from the fabric strips and the weight of the jacket. On the other hand, if you try to shrink a section during blocking, it will probably "grow" when worn, and look baggy. But don't worry too much about a too-large piece: you can easily stitch along the corrected lines and cut it to shape (see the information in "Cutting knitted blocks" below).

To shape a section according to your pattern, multiply the dimensions of the section by your gauge, then increase or decrease as necessary (for more on shaping, see the facing page). I save complicated stitch patterns, like those worked in multiples of eight stitches over 16 rows, for simple rectangular pieces.

Remember that $\frac{1}{4}$ in. of all the section edges will be seam allowances. If you like decorative increases and decreases, work them inside the seam allowance so they will show on the finished garment.

If you're not sure you have enough yarn to complete both a right and left section for your jacket, divide the yarn in half and knit both sections at the same time with separate balls of yarn. If you run out of yarn, you can change the size of the section and any adjoining sections that the change affects.

Cutting knitted blocks—Instead of knitting pieces to shape, you can knit simple squares or rectangles by hand or machine, then sew and cut

continuity of the garment. So after sorting your leftover yarns into color groups, you may want to choose yarns for your jacket that are all variations of the same color, but different in weight, fiber content, and finish, to give your garment depth and texture. Most of my jackets require about 2 lbs. of yarn. You can supplement your leftovers with new yarn, especially for the larger sections on the sleeves.

Arrange the skeins of yarn on the sections of your pattern, and experiment with contrasting textures. Try bulky yarn next to fine, cotton next

to mohair, wool crepe next to worsted acrylic. Place favorite or expensive yarns center back, center front, or on the outside of the sleeves, where they will have the most impact. You can put fine yarn next to bulky yarn because the fabric strips sewn between the pieces support each section independently.

Generally speaking, a yard of worsted-weight yarn will knit around a square inch of your pattern. Sometimes the yarn quantity determines where you can use it, since a partial skein may produce only two small sections. Yarn

the pieces to shape. This method is quicker and will eliminate much of the worry about calculating gauges for each stitch. However, it will require more yarn. For example, if you need two triangular sections in the same yarn and stitch pattern, knit one rectangular block combining them, then stitch and cut diagonally. But first, check to see how the stitch will look reversed (some stitch patterns look the same upside down, while others can look completely different).

After blocking the knitted piece with steam, mark or trace the shape of each section with pins or fabric pen. You can place the knit on a piece of tissue paper or tear-away stabilizer, if necessary, to help prevent stretching, then stitch around the shapes. Use either an over-lock or zigzag stitch, a couple of rows of straight stitching, or a serger, then cut outside the stitching.

You can also combine the two methods by knitting most of the sections to shape, then cutting and sewing the hard-to-shape areas such as curved necklines, armholes, and sleeves.

Layout as you go—As each section is complete, place it in the correct position on the pattern, much like putting a puzzle together. By viewing the sections in place as they are finished, you may decide to change the size, shape, yarn, or stitch for the remaining sections.

Planning and cutting the strips

For the fabric strips that connect the knitted sections, I always choose Ultrasuede or Ultrasuede Light. They require no edge finishing and provide a rich counterpoint to the texture of the knitted sections. Also, their wide color range helps in finding a cohesive fabric color to tie together many shades of yarn (see the sources at right).

To calculate the amount of fabric you need, first estimate the total length of strips required for your design. Measure the length of all seams

Sources for Ultrasuede by the inch or yard
Send swatches of yarns for color matching.

Classic Cloth
34930 U.S. 19 North
Palm Harbor, FL 34684
(800) 237-7739
$39/yd. or $1.25/in.; ¼ yd. minimum; 64 colors; swatch set, $5.

Field's Fabrics By Mail
1695 44th St. S.E.
Grand Rapids, MI 49508
(800) 67ULTRA
$39.95/yd.; 64 colors; swatch set $10.

Ultrascraps
PO Box 339
Farmington, UT 84025
(801) 451-6361
$38.95/yd.; 30 colors; $5 swatch chart.

Knitting a triangle

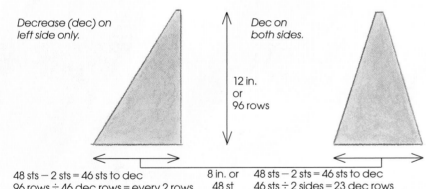

Decrease (dec) on left side only.

Dec on both sides.

12 in. or 96 rows

8 in. or 48 st

48 sts − 2 sts = 46 sts to dec
96 rows ÷ 46 dec rows = every 2 rows (with 4 rows left over—knit at beginning, before first dec)

48 sts − 2 sts = 46 sts to dec
46 sts ÷ 2 sides = 23 dec rows
96 rows ÷ 23 dec rows = dec every 4 rows (with 4 rows left over—knit at beginning, before first dec)

Section D from jacket back

If you divide a complex section into simple shapes and calculate them separately, the section becomes easy to knit.

Knitting fabric to shape

It's a simple task to figure out how to knit a square or rectangular shape. You just multiply the gauge (stitches per in. and rows per in.) by the width and length of the shape. But knitting a triangle is more challenging, because you also have to knit increases or decreases on one or both sides to achieve the shape.

Decreases on one side—Let's start with a simple shape such as the right triangle above left. To knit it from the bottom up, you'll start knitting with the full number of stitches for the width, then decrease evenly on one side, every couple of rows, until you reach the correct length. To knit the same section on the other side of the jacket, just reverse the shaping by working the decreases on the opposite side. You can also knit either section from the top down, starting with two stitches and increasing on one side until you reach the full width.

Decreases on both sides—For a slightly more difficult shape, try the triangle shown at center above, which is shaped evenly on both sides. You'll work the same number of decreases, but divided between two sides of the triangle. A decrease row will happen less often, and you'll work a decrease at each end of that row.

More complicated shapes—Sections such as D on the jacket back (p. 35), can be divided into simple shapes (see the dotted lines at right above) to make them easier to knit. By multiplying each section's dimensions by your gauge, you can shape any straight-sided section.

Here's a tip about knitting shapes in textured patterns that will help the pattern and shaping work together more easily: Let the rhythm of increases or decreases for a shaped piece suggest a stitch pattern for it. For instance, the first example above lends itself to a repeat in multiples of 2, while the second example suggests a pattern with a four-, eight-, or twelve-row repeat.—*T.M.*

Illustrations by Marianne Markey

Lining a knitted cardigan

A patchwork jacket that's pieced with strips of fabric, like the one in the photo on p. 34, needs a full lining to cover all the seam allowances on the inside. I like to use a fairly heavyweight lining fabric such as rayon satin or jacquard, so that the lining can provide some additional support to the body of the jacket.

A properly fitted lining can help to prevent stretching and distortion of the knitted garment during storage and wear. This support is especially important in areas where interfacing was not applied, such as below the waistline and in the sleeves.

Cutting and assembly—To calculate the amount of fabric needed to line your jacket, follow the yardage suggestion on the pattern envelope, or lay out your pattern pieces to estimate the amount. If you trimmed away the ⅝-in. seam allowances to cut the body of the jacket, add them back before cutting the lining, and add 1 in. at the center back for ease. For lengthwise ease, allow an extra ½ in. in addition to the seam allowance.

At the center back of the lining, fold the 1-in. ease allowance toward the right back and machine stitch the resulting pleat in place

A small amount of vertical ease allows the satin lining of this knitted jacket (shown inside out) to provide support to the jacket shell. The lining is pinned, then handsewn to the ribbing on all edges.

twice, 3 in. from the neckline and 1 in. from the lower edge. Assemble the lining, reinforcing the underarm seam by stitching a second time.

Inserting the lining—If your jacket has fabric facings at the neck and fronts, you can sew the lining to the facings by machine, following the instructions in your sewing pattern. For a jacket with ribbed edges, it's best to insert the lining by hand, as follows:

Turn under and press a ⅝-in. hem on all raw edges of the lining. Wrong sides together, slip the lining over the inside-out jacket body and sleeves. Pin or baste the lining to the jacket on all edges, stretching the ribbing to its original width to ease the lining in place.

Hang the jacket on a suit hanger or dress form, both right side out and inside out, to check the drape of both the lining and the shell, as shown at left. Check that the bottom and sleeve hems blouse slightly (about ½ in.) to allow for wearing ease, but fit closely enough to support the knitted shell.

By hand, slip-stitch the lining in place around all edges. I prefer not to tack the lining at the armholes or shoulders, to provide wearing ease. —*T.M.*

seams. Pressing can correct minor distortion caused by sewing, and you will be pleasantly surprised at how forgiving both the suede and knit can be.

With a steam iron, reblock the assembled jacket pieces to the dimensions of your pattern. Sew the shoulder seams, then stabilize the shoulder area and center fronts with a lightweight fusible-knit interfacing such as Stacy's Easy Knit or Dritz Soft 'n' Silky, ironing the interfacing over the sections and pressed-open seam allowances. Even a "sweatery" cardigan will benefit from this extra support, because of it's weight. For a more structured jacket, you can add heavier interfacing, such as horsehair.

Finishing the jacket

After you assemble the jacket shell and before you add the lining (see "Lining a knitted cardigan" at left), try on the jacket with the shoulder pads pinned in place to check the fit and hang. If the garment needs more stability, add additional interfacing.

If you plan to knit single- or double-layer ribbings on the edges of your jacket, you may need to pick up stitches through the fabric strips. Poke a hole with a tapestry needle, pull a loop of yarn through the fabric, and pick it up as a stitch. (For more on ribbing, see *Basics, Threads* No. 48).

Your patchwork jacket is likely to become the foundation of your wardrobe. It's warm, durable, comfortable, and resists wrinkling. It looks great with everything from jeans and tennis shoes to a skirt and heels. But practical reasons aside, once a stranger stops you to ask "Where did you get your jacket?", you can't help but reach for it every time you go out. □

Tamsen McAndrews designs knitted and sewn clothing. Patterns for some of her patchwork knits are available from Tamsen Designs, 6143 28th St. SE, Grand Rapids, MI 49546.

on the pattern pieces that need strips, both between the sections and joining the edges of the pattern pieces. Add an extra ½ in. to each strip for safety. You'll cut the 1-in. strips crosswise (selvage to selvage) on the fabric, so group strips of various lengths together to use the long pieces economically.

If you're adding in-seam pockets to your jacket, follow a sewing pattern. You'll need to add width to the fabric strips at the pocket opening so the lining fabric won't show (I add ½ in. to the strip in front and an additional 1-in. strip in back).

The quickest way to cut the Ultrasuede is with a rotary cutter and clear ruler. You can also mark the suede on the wrong side with a pen and straightedge at 1-in. intervals, then cut with scissors.

You'll also need to determine the sequence for assembling the strips and sections, and label them numerically (see p. 35). Assemble the short strips first, so they'll be covered by another strip.

Assembling the sections

After cutting the strips, you're ready to start assembling the sections. Beginning

with seam No. 1 on the garment back, place the appropriate fabric strip along the edge of one section right sides together, and stitch in a ¼-in. seam with the fabric on the bottom and the knitting on top. This will help keep the fabric from shifting and will allow you to feed the knit evenly, which helps to prevent stretching. Sew the adjoining section to the opposite edge of the fabric strip.

After each seam is stitched, press it open before adding the next section. Don't trim the excess fabric at the ends until you sew the overlapping

Knitting Strip by Strip

You can forget the gauge and save the sweater's shaping for later

by Deborah Newton

i find inspiration for knitwear everywhere. But sometimes it takes a long time to figure out how to use some of the ideas that most excite me. Recently, a South American knitted hat with bird motifs (at right) and a book about African strip-woven textiles challenged my ingenuity.

It struck me that knitting a sweater in strips might be the way to go. Strips are quick and fun to knit. Any kind of patterning is appropriate: solid-colored, multicolored, textured, even lace—whatever appeals to you. The strips can all be the same width, or they can vary, as mine do. Gauge isn't critical, but take possible stretch into account. Because you can change your patterns or colors so often and the pieces are narrow and quickly completed, even a large project like a coat holds your interest and doesn't become bulky or heavy until the finishing stages.

Swatch with the yarn you're planning to use to see what sort of garment will be appropriate. I swatched with a worsted-weight yarn that had the color palette I desired, Reynolds' "Paterna," and decided that a boxy, oversized, short coat would be ideal. That was the only decision I made before I began knitting strips of varied width, trusting that I could find ways to assemble them into a garment later. The result is the sweater shown on p. 41.

After knitting all the strips you think you'll need for the body, experiment with different layouts. When you settle on a design, sew the strips together and complete the neck and shoulder shaping as I've described on p. 43. Then make the sleeves, and sew them in. Finishing touches include a collar and decorative edgings that also add stability. I found every stage of this process exhilarating, and I hope you'll give this method a try too.

Knitting strips

Choose your own pattern(s), texture, and yarn. Whatever your yarn choice, use a needle size that gives you a tension that feels good for the type of garment you'd like to make.

A firm, dense fabric is well-suited to a coat, but if you want a drapier garment, try a looser gauge or a finer yarn. Assembly is easier if your strips are an even width from top to bottom, but if you want wavy strips, try working with different textured patterns or mixing yarns of different weights. One thing you should keep in mind is that the more strips you knit, the more seams you will have to sew.

Pattern selection—When you knit strips with motifs or other patterning, you need to decide if you want the designs to line up horizontally. To avoid what I'd consider an unflattering horizontal accent, I decided to work toward an ethnic, patch-

Knitting patterned strips is fun. As on the South American hat that inspired her, Deborah Newton alternated background and pattern colors in each motif block. The green she wanted for the "solid" areas didn't exist, so she blended two shades, as described in Basics, Threads No. 45, p. 16. Mattress stitch between strips makes a flat, nearly invisible seam. Newton also explains how to plan neck and shoulder shaping for a perfect fit.

From *Threads* magazine (February 1993) 45:51-55

How to lay out a strip-knitted coat

The strip widths on your sweater can vary, as they do on the coat shown below, but the back and fronts need to be exactly the same width, excluding a double-breasted underlap. Knitting two strips in each pattern makes this easier, but you can also just knit an extra strip to add to the narrower section. Edgings are not shown. See p. 43 for shaping the neck curve and shoulders.

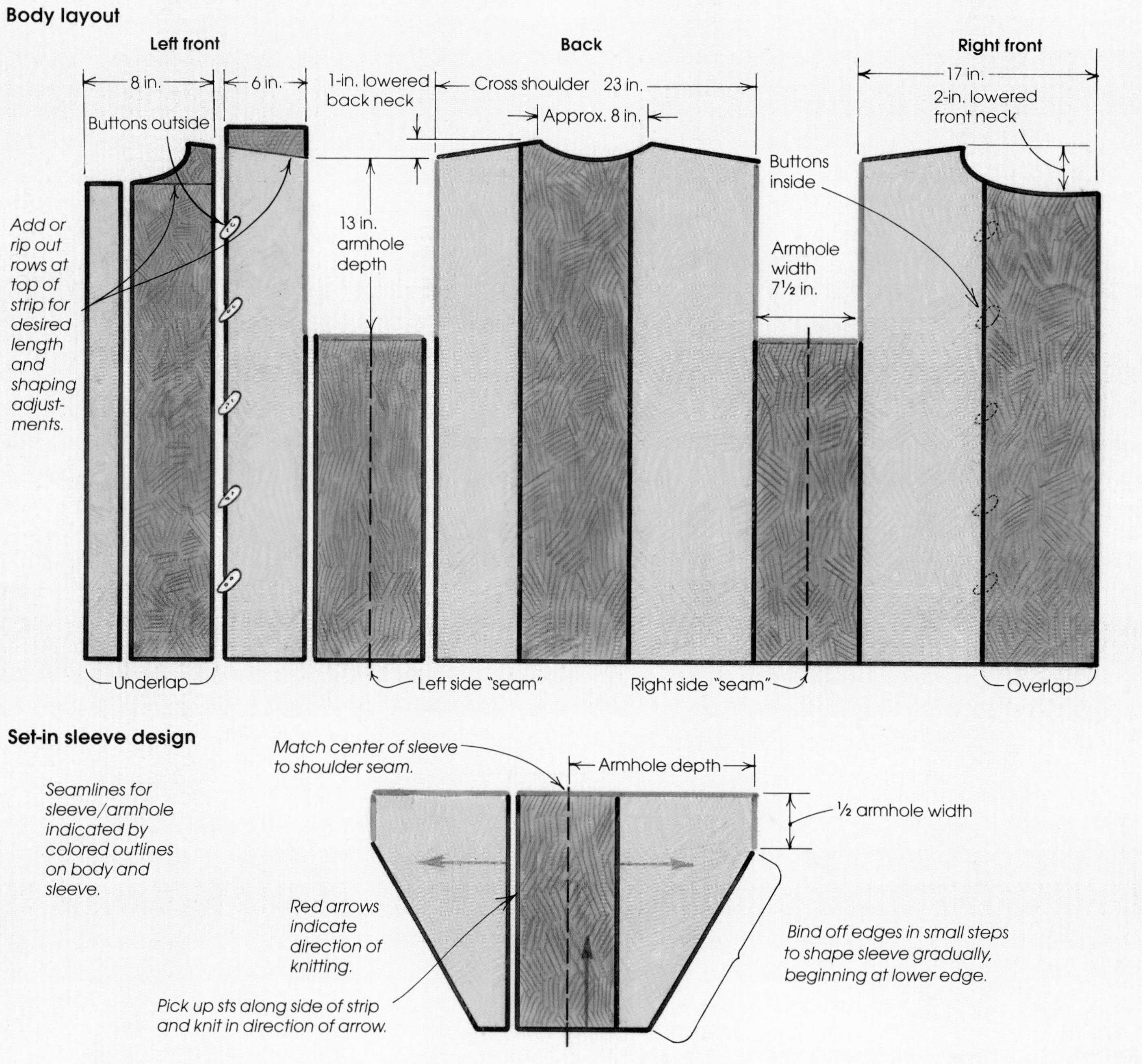

Body layout

Left front

8 in.

6 in.

Buttons outside

Add or rip out rows at top of strip for desired length and shaping adjustments.

Underlap

1-in. lowered back neck

13 in. armhole depth

Left side "seam"

Back

Cross shoulder 23 in.

Approx. 8 in.

Buttons inside

Armhole width 7½ in.

Right side "seam"

Right front

17 in.

2-in. lowered front neck

Overlap

Set-in sleeve design

Seamlines for sleeve/armhole indicated by colored outlines on body and sleeve.

Match center of sleeve to shoulder seam.

Armhole depth

½ armhole width

Red arrows indicate direction of knitting.

Pick up sts along side of strip and knit in direction of arrow.

Bind off edges in small steps to shape sleeve gradually, beginning at lower edge.

---

work effect with the motifs staggered. Since each motif was a different width and height, I decided to break them up with areas of solid color that would also add continuity to the overall design. I just knit those areas to different lengths too, being sure that there was enough solid color at the top of each strip to allow for shaping. That way, no matter how I eventually laid out the strips, nothing would line up exactly. If your preference

is for a more symmetrical effect, you'll need to plan the lengths of the parts of your strips more carefully than I did.

Strip length—I suggest making all the body strips the full length from hem to shoulder since you won't know which will be involved in neck and shoulder shaping as you knit them. It's easier to rip out the tops of the strips that require shaping—since very little knitting needs

to be added back to each—than it is to knit several more inches onto many of your strips. While I was knitting strips, I also decided to make four shorter ones—probably for the sleeves, although I hadn't yet determined sleeve shape or style.

You don't have to be too precise about the exact length of your strips, but if you're working in many colors, begin and end each with a section of solid color. Besides giving the design continuity, this

A knitted coat may seem like a daunting project. But when you knit it as a series of narrow strips with whatever color or texture patterning you like, the knitting proceeds rapidly. When you've made enough strips for your garment's circumference, you get to play with different ways to arrange them.

Photo by Susan Kahn

Underarm bulk can be avoided by setting in sleeves. Newton picked up stitches along a patterned center strip and knit toward the underarm, shaping with small bind-off steps.

makes lengthening or shortening and shaping easier later on.

After weaving in the final color ends (if needed), steam each strip to block the knitting if the fiber allows. Only after blocking can you measure your strips accurately to determine whether any need to be lengthened or shortened. It's easy to lengthen those that are a little short: just undo the bind-off and knit a few more rows (to shorten, unravel a few rows). Then bind off again and resteam.

Layout

If you thought knitting was the fun part, you're in for a treat because planning how your strips will fit together into a garment is even more exciting. I have two suggestions about this stage: Don't rush it, and try lots of options. You may find that setting one or more strips into the garment upside down is surprisingly pleasing, as I did on the right front of my coat. The front and back need to be the same width (don't count underlaps). If your strips are all different widths, you might find this challenging. I knit two strips of each pattern, which gave me enough symmetry to lay out equal fronts and back. Another solution is to knit an extra strip the width you need to fill out the narrower side if no other layout works.

Shaping the armhole—When I started playing with my strips, I decided to use two of the shorter ones for side panels, creating a shaped armhole so that I

would be able to make set-in sleeves. Shaped armholes make a sweater fit better by narrowing the cross-shoulder width and eliminating excess bulk at the underarm. So I lengthened two of the short "sleeve" strips to fill in from underarm to hem and was left with only two sleeve strips.

Front closures—The next thing to decide is how you want the coat fronts to meet and close. You could choose a symmetrical center front with button band and buttonhole band knit later. An asymmetrical closure is also a nice touch to consider. At first I planned to button my coat at the left side front, with the two fronts meeting. But as the assembly progressed, I began to think that the heavy fabric would be better supported and would hang straighter and button more securely with a double-breasted closure (as in the drawing on p. 40). So I knitted an extra two panels—one patterned and one solid and very narrow—for the edge of the left front to produce an underlap.

Sewing the strips together

Once you've decided the body layout, it's time to sew all the strips together. Start at the bottom and seam toward the top, but leave the last 2 to 3 in. unsewn on the pieces that will require shaping—if you've decided to add shaping—for shoulder and front and back necklines. See "Planning neck and shoulder shaping" on the facing page for general informa-

tion about how to produce these shapes. Take out the bound-off edges on these strips one at a time, remove as many rows as necessary, slip the stitches onto a needle, and complete the shaping you've calculated. When all the strips have been shaped, complete the seams. Then join the shoulders.

My favorite seam technique for knits is mattress stitch (see *Threads* No. 42, p. 18), because it's strong, stretchy, and nearly invisible; and since you work from the right side, you can always see how the patterns are lining up. Besides, I enjoy doing it. You don't need to work special selvage stitches to prepare for it, but be aware that you lose the edge stitches of each strip into the selvage.

Whenever you sew long seams, place markers every 4 in. on each piece, matching them as you sew. If the row gauges of the pieces are similar, the seams will go together nearly row for row. But when joining a piece with a tighter row gauge, occasionally take an extra bar from the tighter piece so that the strips will end up the same length.

Sleeves

To make shaped sleeves like the ones on my coat, pick up stitches (see *Threads* No. 42, p. 20) along the sides of a sleeve-length strip, one stitch for each row. Then knit as shown in the drawing on p. 40, binding off gradually in small steps—beginning at the cuff end—to shape the sleeve sides. Note that the last section to be bound off at the top side of each sleeve matches half of the armhole width; and half of the upper-sleeve width matches the armhole depth, as shown in the photo above left.

To calculate the dimensions of the sleeve's side panels, start with your row gauge (rows/in.). To plan the number of rows that you'll need, subtract half the width of the central band from the armhole depth and multiply the result by the row gauge. So that the cuff will be wide enough, you must knit several rows straight (use the row gauge to determine the number). To find out how many stitches must remain, multiply the stitch gauge (sts/in.) by half the armhole width. Subtract this number from the total number of picked-up stitches to give you the number of stitches to divide evenly into the stair-step bind-off for the underarm shaping. Three or four stitches bound off per step is about right. To find out the number of rows between each step, subtract the number of full-length rows from the total number of rows. Then see whether 3 or 4 goes more evenly into the total to determine the bind-

Planning neck and shoulder shaping

Whether a sweater is knit of strips or in back and front pieces, you need to lower and curve the back and front necklines to allow for body contours and good fit. A straight back neck bound off even with the top of the shoulders often lies in a lump of fabric at the base of the collar—particularly if the fabric is heavy. I plot neck and shoulder shaping row for row and stitch for stitch on graph paper. You'll find this particularly helpful with a strip garment since the shaping will involve several strips at different places. A medium-size back neck is generally about 7 to 8 in. wide (as is the front, but deeper). But each garment may be a little different. Measure the back neck of a sweater that fits and has a similar weight fabric.

Calculate the number of stitches you'll need for your neck width. The rest of the back stitches are divided evenly between the two shoulders. The front shoulders will have exactly the same number of stitches as the back, and for a symmetrical garment the same number of stitches will comprise both front and back necklines. (Since the front of my coat is asymmetrical, the front necklines are shaped differently, as you can see in the drawing on p. 40.

A warm outerwear garment like a coat generally has a fairly high neckline, and so I decided to lower the center-front neckline only 2 in., rather than the 2½ to 3 in. I would normally choose for a crewneck sweater.

For a close fit at back neck, I seldom lower it more than 1 in. But a slight lowering and curve is important to fit the body's contours.

Back neck and shoulders— I usually bind off the middle ½ to ¾ of the stitches all at once. From now on, you'll have to work each side of the neck curve separately. First, bind off two or three shallow stair-steps, as shown at left. Each step is about 1 in. wide. When you've taken as many stitches out of the curve as you desire, work the edge straight until the piece is done.

Neckline shaping for a pullover or cardigan

For a well-fitted neckline, use bind-off steps to shape the curve. Back curve is shallower than front, but both have same number of stitches. Shoulders are bound off in steps for a natural slope.

Shaping the back neck and shoulders

Shoulder and neck shaping occur simultaneously.

Shoulder stitch count (same for all four pieces)

Shoulder stitch count (same for all four pieces)

3 or 4 even steps

1 in.

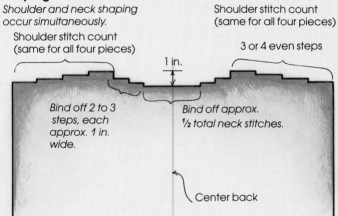

Bind off 2 to 3 steps, each approx. 1 in. wide.

Bind off approx. ½ total neck stitches.

Center back

Back shoulder shaping often begins at the same time or within two rows of back-neck shaping. Depending on shoulder width and the number of rows it takes to work 1 in., I divide the stitches evenly into three or four groups and bind off that number at the beginning of each armhole edge. When I've bound off the last group, no back stitches remain.

Front neck and shoulders— Since the front neck begins lower than the back neck, the curve must be more gradual, so bind off ⅓ to ½ the number of front neck stitches. Work more and smaller bind-off steps along each side of the front neck than those on the back neck. Then decrease 1 st every other row on each neck edge until only the shoulder stitches remain. Work even until the front is just short of the four to six rows required for the shoulder shaping. Complete shoulder shaping just as for the back, being sure to begin each side at the armhole edge. —D.N.

Shaping the front neck and shoulders

Neck shaping is completed before shoulder shaping.

Work even until length equals back, minus shoulder shaping.

2 to 3 in.

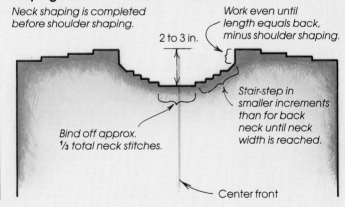

Stair-step in smaller increments than for back neck until neck width is reached.

Bind off approx. ⅓ total neck stitches.

Center front

off frequency and amount.

Sew the sleeve tops into the armholes, then sew the sleeve seams. Your coat is now almost finished.

Edgings and collar

Knitted coats and cardigans tend to drape more evenly with edgings added to the front opening and hem. Garter stitch (knit every row), which I used, is an ideal, noncurling edging for stockinette fabric. Seed stitch, in which knit and purl stitches alternate in checkerboard fashion, is another good choice since it doesn't curl either. Ribbed bands will pull your edges in much more than garter or seed stitch, which may be exactly what you want.

To keep all of the edgings firm, use a needle that's two sizes smaller than the needle you used for the strips. And to ensure that the edgings join the main fabric firmly, pick up the first row with a needle that's about two sizes smaller than the edging needle.

This was the first garment I'd ever knit without planning every step carefully in advance. And I had so much fun with it that I'm eager to try another. □

Deborah Newton, author of Designing Knitwear *(The Taunton Press, 1992), is a contributing editor to* Threads.

Illustrations by Clarke

Norwegian Sweaters
Finish your knitting with a flourish of embroidery

by Nancy Carney

twenty-five years ago I went to a traditional Norwegian wedding. The bride wore a green wool gathered skirt and matching vest with pewter clasps. Everything was embroidered with fine wool in Jacobean-style motifs. After the ceremony I stood behind her for the official pictures and couldn't help but bend down and lift the hem of her garment—a picture photographed for posterity. I was enchanted by her traditional ethnic gown and, later that evening, by the beautiful wool *luskoften*, knitted jackets and pullovers with embroidered wool edges or bibs called "felt," that some of the guests wore.

A few months later, I discovered Snowflake Kits, a Norwegian mail-order business that supplied yarns, pewter clasps, and even embroidery felt kits. I still attract admiring stares when I wear the first sweater I made from one of their packages. Such durability of both the Triplex wool yarn and the ethnic design has led me to knit and design primarily within this style. In addition, my family of platinum blonds can tolerate this particular wool touching their skin, whereas anything else causes rashes or discomfort.

As the years went on, Snowflake kits carried fewer and fewer of the traditional designs with the embroidered edges, and I began to design more and more of my own. Last autumn they discontinued them altogether, and when I wrote in protest, they responded that such goods are no longer fashionable in Norway. They will still supply the patterns for their original embroidered sweater kits, however (see "Sources" on p. 47), and I recommend them highly. I have never ordered Norwegian wool from anyone but Snowflake because I find their quality and service so superior.

Knitting the sweater

Anyone who knits, embroiders, and sews moderately well can make the sweaters shown on the facing page. First you knit a sweater. Then you embroider the wool bands to trim it, and finally you sew them to the sweater. I always knit in the round, in the Scandinavian manner, as explained in the drawings on p. 46. To figure out how many stitches you need to go around the body, knit a patterned swatch, count the number of stitches per inch, and multiply this figure by the desired number of inches around. Similarly, the number of rows per inch will tell you how many rows your sweater's length will require.

You can use just about any yarn for the knitted base. As in all knitting, the gauge is the important thing. However, to take the weight of the embroidery and its facing, I don't recommend sport, or 3-ply, yarn. The 2/4-ply Triplex is a bit lighter than worsted weight. But because the knitting is patterned throughout, the finished garment's thickness is like a worsted-weight sweater with a gauge of six stitches to the inch.

Perhaps the most traditional pattern is the "crossed ski" design. This looks like large Xs across the chest; the large star pattern at far right in the photo is also traditional. In addition, knitters put a pattern or two right above the body and sleeve ribbing (or above the embroidered cuff if the sleeve is unribbed), and at the sleeve shoulder. These are geometric and are usually a series of smaller patterns separated by a repeating border. Scandinavian knitters also like to use "snowflake" dots throughout the unpatterned parts of their sweaters. This extra wool produces a thermal effect, making the entire garment warmer. The frequency of dots can vary, as shown in the center drawing on p. 46, but the closer they are, the warmer the sweater will be. If you add a contrasting color at the tops of the sleeves and shoulders, you can pick it up again in the embroidery.

Knit the sleeves on a short circular needle or five double-pointed needles, from the lower edge up, as shown in the right-hand drawing, p. 46. Include an additional half-inch for a facing at the top; then cast off. The sleeve will look short because the sweater has a dropped shoulder. To decide how long to knit the sleeve, hold the completed body piece against the wearer to see approximately where the dropped shoulder will be. Measure from wrist to this point for the sleeve length.

Cutting the sweater

After the three pieces are completed, you cut the body tube down the front for a cardigan, or, for a pullover, as far as is necessary to insert the embroidered chest panel. For a cardigan, the cutting line is at the end-of-round; but for a pullover, the end-of-round is placed under one of the sleeves. Before cutting, always run four lines of machine stitching (I prefer zigzag, but straightstitch is fine), two on either side of the cutting line to prevent raveling.

To form a crew neck, use a plate to chalk mark a balanced arc 7 in. wide and 2 in. deep for the front. I machine stitch before cutting, as shown in the lower drawing on p. 46. Then I trim off the excess. Since the garment will have a stand-up collar, I leave about an inch of the knitting above the stitching for an extra interfacing. So, at this point, I am careful not to cut away any further than the height of the planned collar.

Next I make the sleeve cuts the depth of the top of the sleeve width. I set my sleeves in by machine, allowing the half-inch facing to extend beyond the sewing line on the inside. Then I hem it over the raw edge. Some people like to set the sleeves in an inch or two so the shoulder isn't as dropped. To make a partially set-in sleeve, sew, then cut a rectangle one to two inches into the body tube for the depth of the sleeve; be sure to make the sleeves correspondingly longer. I prefer the traditional dropped shoulder style; and, besides, I hate to waste any of my knitting. If you're new to cutting knitting, try thinking of the pieces as expensive yard goods. ⇨

Norwegian sweaters are knit as tubes, then cut open for cardigan or pullover styles. Embroidered "felts" trim the openings. (Photo by

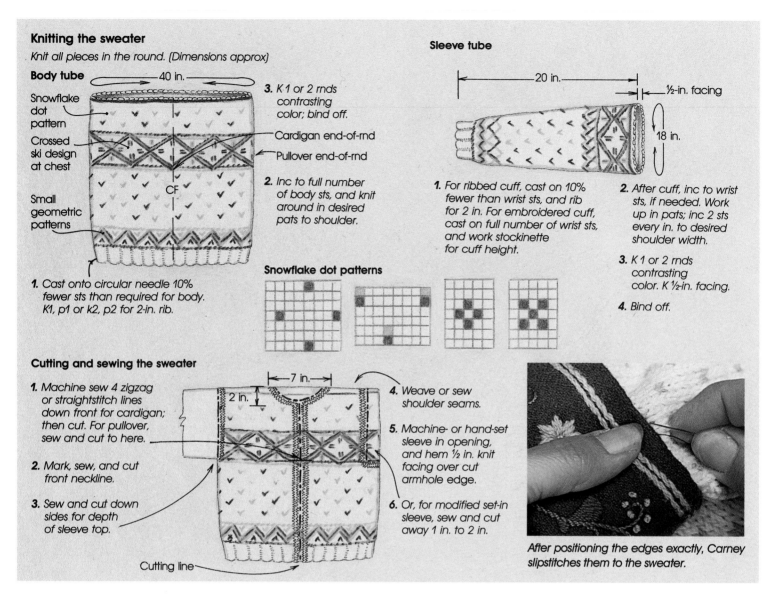

Knitting the sweater

Knit all pieces in the round. (Dimensions approx)

Body tube

← 40 in. →

- Snowflake dot pattern
- Crossed ski design at chest
- Small geometric patterns

CF

3. K 1 or 2 rnds contrasting color; bind off.

- Cardigan end-of-rnd
- Pullover end-of-rnd

2. Inc to full number of body sts, and knit around in desired pats to shoulder.

1. Cast onto circular needle 10% fewer sts than required for body. K1, p1 or k2, p2 for 2-in. rib.

Sleeve tube

← 20 in. →   ← ½-in. facing

18 in.

1. For ribbed cuff, cast on 10% fewer than wrist sts, and rib for 2 in. For embroidered cuff, cast on full number of wrist sts, and work stockinette for cuff height.

2. After cuff, inc to wrist sts, if needed. Work up in pats; inc 2 sts every in. to desired shoulder width.

3. K 1 or 2 rnds contrasting color. K ½-in. facing.

4. Bind off.

Snowflake dot patterns

Cutting and sewing the sweater

← 7 in. →

2 in.

1. Machine sew 4 zigzag or straightstitch lines down front for cardigan; then cut. For pullover, sew and cut to here.

2. Mark, sew, and cut front neckline.

3. Sew and cut down sides for depth of sleeve top.

Cutting line

4. Weave or sew shoulder seams.

5. Machine- or hand-set sleeve in opening, and hem ½ in. knit facing over cut armhole edge.

6. Or, for modified set-in sleeve, sew and cut away 1 in. to 2 in.

After positioning the edges exactly, Carney slipstitches them to the sweater.

You can do all of this shaping by hand, and for a well-finished sweater, you would even weave the shoulder seam so that it is invisible. To do that, you have to unravel the shoulder bind-off to give you open loops. Then you graft the loops together, as shown in *Basics, Threads* No. 34. I am a lazy finisher, and so I simply sew all my seams by machine.

Embroidering the trim

Nowhere have I found a detailed description of what to use for embroidery materials or an account of how to attach the embroidered trims to the sweater. Even my original Snowflake kit simply told me to do the embroidery in any stitches and colors I desired and then, "Affix to knitted garment." From that first sweater I was on my own, so I treated my embroidered cuffs, front edgings, and collar as if I were tailoring a blazer.

Today, I buy a good grade, closely woven wool for my embroidery base. I still prefer the traditional black and usually use Pendleton wool. A cardigan generally requires a half-yard of 60-in.-wide material for the embroidery and facings. I also like to run a wool-covered cording around the outside of the collars, cuffs, and edgings.

I sketch most of my designs on any available paper first, as shown on the facing page. After looking at many pictures of traditional Scandinavian clothing, you will develop a feel for what is ethnic. I have always wanted to go beyond this traditional point but have only just begun. You could think about embroidering Jacobean, Native American, or Oriental designs; and you might vary the knitted base to include a greater variety of yarns and give the garment a homespun, dressy, or eclectic feel.

It is difficult for me to embroider with wool yarn on wool and not shade the individual designs with long-and-short stitches, but I have not seen this done in any of the Scandinavian sources. They seem to use mostly satin stitch, stem stitch, and back stitch to work somewhat geometric designs, often repeated along a curving baseline. Embroidered areas are filled in with bright

wool; sometimes one or more of the colors will be the exact shade of the knitting wool. Usually the knitted sweater looks dull in comparison to the embroidery.

First I decide the width, length, and shape of the embroidered pieces and make a paper pattern for each. I make the collar and front edges of a cardigan or pullover the same width, usually about 2½ in. A bib front usually extends 8 to 10 in., and it may flare toward the bottom. I measure the sweater base carefully to determine the length of cardigan fronts and collar, which will be set after the front edges have been applied. At first I used sewing patterns to help me with the collar shape. Embroidered cuffs are usually the same width as the other pieces, but occasionally, I'll design them twice as deep. Then on the patterns, I draw a sinuous connecting line throughout the design. Next I begin to play with the basic Scandinavian shapes along this baseline until I have something that appeals to me. I usually leave about a half-inch of breathing space around the design.

When finished, I transfer the design onto the Pendleton wool with the vertical cardigan edgings set along the crossgrain and the center back of the collar on grain. I use dressmaker's carbon first, and then go over this with white ink. The more definite the transferred markings, the easier it will be to embroider; but I have occasionally just sketched on the Pendleton wool with chalk. Be sure to leave room for a ⅝-in. seam allowance all around all the pieces.

I do most of my embroidery in wool yarns. I buy some crewel thread and usually unply some of the Triplex I have used for knitting. The embroidered colors and the sweater body then match exactly. Because the plies of the Norwegian yarn are spun more firmly than American yarn, unplying is easy. Each ply is just a hair thinner than crewel yarn. I work highlights within the design in pearl cotton and cotton floss of varying weights. I like the slight contrasting sheen that the cotton gives. In most of my designs, I add a bright gold pearl cotton (or doubled floss) line along the edges for accent. I usually work it in stem stitch, but sometimes I make the line zigzag or use a variation of simple couching. (See *Basics*, *Threads* No. 34 for some embroidery stitches.) I also use the cotton floss for French knots and the smaller leaves and flowers.

Assembling and finishing

After completing the embroidery and cutting out the pieces, I steam iron them flat at the same time I am steaming the knitted body. I cut an interfacing (stiff Pellon or hair canvas) and a facing (of the Pendleton wool), both the same size as the embroidered pieces. Then I cover cording with a bias strip of the same color wool or a complementary color. I usually use the same color fabric for the facing and the embroidery base. Next, I baste the interfacing to the embroidered pieces. For the pullover, I assemble collar and bib facing and sew about an inch of the "felt" collar-bib seam at its front edge. Then I attach the covered cording, right sides together, along the outer edges of the pieces, aligning seam allowances. Finally, I sew on the facing over the piping, right sides together. I clip corners and curves, turn the pieces, and steam them flat once again. I allow them to dry thoroughly while I finish cutting and assembling the sweater.

With someone wearing the knitted base, or using a dressmaker's dummy, I fold under the seam allowances and pin the unpiped edges of the embroidered pieces to the sweater to make sure everything is positioned exactly. This step is crucial for collars and the embroidered bib fronts of pullovers; they must be straight and balance exactly. You might need to trim away a bit more of the knitted garment, but be very careful. If you trim too much, you cannot put it back. I do not run more machine stitching before doing this additional trimming because all the cut edges will immediately be covered and protected by the embroidered, faced pieces, so they won't have a chance to ravel.

Next I slipstitch the embroidered pieces onto the knitted base by hand, as shown in the photo on the facing page. I sew the pewter clasps or buttons onto the embroidered fronts before finally slipstitching the facing inside. This way the facing covers the thread and knots.

Remember, even after you have decided upon your embroidery and knitting designs, the time required for this garment is the equivalent of a patterned-throughout sweater and a crewel pillow or two, *plus* partial tailoring of a suit jacket. If your design is timeless and you use the best materials available to you, your sweater will withstand hard use for several decades. You will probably want to wear it that long too.□

Nancy Carney lives in Newtown, CT, where she designs gardens and sweaters and teaches knitting.

Sources

Nordic Fiber Arts
4 Cutts Rd.
Durham, NH 03824
Yarns, patterns and kits, pewter buttons and clasps; color cards $5.

Norsk Fjord Fiber
PO Box 271-T
Lexington, GA 30648
Suitable yarns, wide assortment of pewter buttons and clasps, sweater kits, tools, and books; catalog $1.

Snowflake Kits
N-1315 Nesøya
Norway
Triplex wool yarn (50g skeins) in beautiful jewel colors. Variety of pewter buttons and clasps. Pricing reasonable; accepts personal checks in U.S. funds; yarn prices lower in bulk.

Books

Bohn, Annichen Sibbern, *Norwegian Sweater Designs.* Oslo, Norway: Grøndahl and Son, 1965. *Excellent plates of antique knitted garments and their pattern designs, updates the* luskoften.

Dale Yarn Company's *Knit Your Own Norwegian Sweaters.* New York: Dover Publications, 1974. *Traditional designs and methods.*

Snook, Barbara, *Embroidery Stitches.* New York: St. Martin's Press, 1986. *Excellent stitch dictionary.*

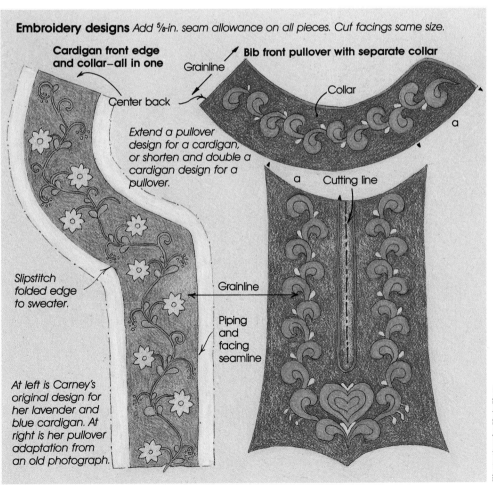

Embroidery designs Add ⅝-in. seam allowance on all pieces. Cut facings same size.

Cardigan front edge and collar—all in one

Bib front pullover with separate collar

Grainline

Center back

Collar

Extend a pullover design for a cardigan, or shorten and double a cardigan design for a pullover.

a

a Cutting line

Slipstitch folded edge to sweater.

Grainline

Piping and facing seamline

At left is Carney's original design for her lavender and blue cardigan. At right is her pullover adaptation from an old photograph.

Illustrations by Chris Clapp

Sensorama Sweaters

Hidden noisemakers and embroidered details that kids will love

by Wendy Keele

adults are satisfied to admire a beautifully knitted sweater, but just looking does not satisfy children. They want to touch the sweater, play with it, and generally explore it. You can capitalize on this natural curiosity by knitting embellished sweaters for your child. Pom-poms, jingle bells, squeakers, rattles, appliqués, buttons, bows, sequins, and knitted flaps are just some of the many embellishments that can make a child's sweater fun to wear.

My middle child Greg is crazy about dinosaurs and at 22 months started saying "stegso" for the stegosaurus dinosaurs in his books. That was my design idea for his "Stegosaurus Sweater." Holidays also suggest ideas. When Ben, our oldest child, wanted to be a ghost for Halloween, making a ghost costume didn't sound like much fun to me, so we agreed on a ghost sweater instead. (See both sweaters at left.)

Balls and balloons seem to appeal to most babies and toddlers, and they're perfect places to hide an additional sensory delight. At just 10 months, my youngest child Marcia knew that many of my sweaters contain hidden squeakers, and she'd pat any raised motif looking for them. She would beam with delight and satisfaction when she found the elusive squeak.

Planning a sweater

I recommend a simple drop-shoulder body style because it provides the maximum design space. Construction is easy, and the simple lines allow you to emphasize design rather than construction. With no sleeve cap shaping it's easy to continue the design from the body to the sleeves. You can use a commercial drop-shoulder pattern, or you can design your own using one of the excellent books listed on p. 52.

When I want to vary my basic pattern, I change the neck treatments. But generally, I prefer a crew neck because my designs usually cover a large portion of the sweater front. If the design is located mainly at the hem, a placket neck treatment is an excellent way to move a viewer's eyes from the design up to the child's face.

There are appropriate uses for all fibers and weights of yarn. Generally, the sweater body should be constructed with plain yarns because the embellishment should be the focal point. Novelty and variegated yarns are usually better for the embellished details. But if the design is very simple, a tweedy or textured yarn might be needed to add more interest to the sweater.

Fiber type will vary depending on the use of the sweater, the amount of money you want to spend, the color selection of the yarn, and the child's age. For example, I used an inexpensive acrylic yarn for Ben's "Ghost Sweater" because it was such a seasonal garment. On the other hand, for Greg's "Stegosaurus Sweater" I selected a 100% wool. I wanted this to be a special sweater, and I liked the available colors. I would have preferred a washable wool but could not find the colors I wanted, so I sacrificed easy care for the right colors.

Try to keep the yarn weight in proportion to the sweater size. If you are knitting a size 1 baby sweater, sport weight is more appropriate than bulky. Ben's "Ghost Sweater" is worsted weight. I could have

Keele's embellished children's sweaters are as much fun to make as they are to wear. While each technique is relatively simple, the cumulative effect is extraordinary. (Photo by Susan Kahn)

Making circus elephants

Here's how to make the trunks and ears to embellish the intarsia-knit "Elephant Pyramid Sweater," shown at left and on page 64. Work the lower edge diamonds in intarsia. For the other trim, knit a triangular flag, embroider an aida cloth pennant to appliqué on top of the flag (hide a squeaker under the appliquéd flag), and couch a yarn staff in place. Sew on various types of sequins and "goo-goo" eyes; embroider the mouths and swiss darn the back cloths (or work them in intarsia); and knot on short fringes. The tails are three-strand braids.

Trunks—With worsted-weight grey yarn and two size 8 double-pointed needles, cast on 3 sts for I-cord: K3, slide the sts to the other end of the needle, pull the yarn firmly across the back, and k3 again. Repeat until the piece of I-cord is 3½ in. long. K3 tog. Make three trunks.

Sew the trunks to the sweater with the bottom elephants' trunks curling around each other and the top elephant's trunk holding the pennant.

Ears—With variegated worsted-weight yarn and size 8 needles, cast on 5 (7) sts; work 2 rows of stockinette st. Then inc 1 st each edge every other row 2 times—9 (11) sts. Work one row even. Dec 1 st each edge on next row—7 (9) sts. Work one row even. Bind off. Make two ears of each size.

With worsted-weight grey yarn and two size 8 double-pointed needles, pick up one st on lower right-hand edge of ear. Cast on 3 sts, for a total of 4 sts on needle. *K2, k2 tog. Do not turn work. Pick up another stitch from ear with left end of needle. Slide sts to other end of needle and pull yarn across back. Transfer empty needle to right hand.* Repeat from *-* until you have knitted an edge around the curved section of the ear. Last row: slide sts to other end of needle, k3 tog.

The larger ears are for the elephant on top of the pyramid. Sew straight edge of ears to sweater. Tack the upper right or left corner of each ear to the sweater so they don't stand out. —W.K.

In "Elephant Pyramid," Wendy Keele uses intarsia for the elephant bodies and embellishes them with knit ears and trunks, embroidery, appliqué, and sewn-on eyes and sequins.

Schematic of "Elephant Pyramid" sweater

Draw sweater shape roughly to scale and block in design areas.
Gauge: 4 sts and 6 rows = 1 in.

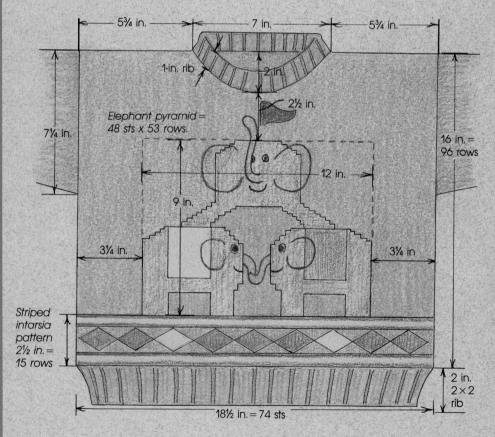

Fit design idea onto knitter's graph paper blocked out for desired number of stitches and rows. Shapes will look blocky when redrawn to exact grid rectangles.

used a sport weight yarn, but I wanted the sweater to knit up quickly, so the heavier weight was a better choice. Greg's "Stegosaurus Sweater" is a size 3, so I wanted the finer gauge of sport weight to give me more stitches and thus a more detailed design.

Developing the design idea

Next comes the really fun part of designing your child's sweater. You have all the information you need for the mechanics of constructing the sweater—size, style, and yarn. Now you can think of ways to make your design idea fun for you to knit and enjoyable for your child to wear. Evaluate your skills as a knitter. If you are a beginner, consider knitting a plain sweater and sewing on or embroidering all the embellishments later. If you know how to work intarsia (see the top drawing, page 52), you can knit in the intarsia motif and then add the embellishments.

Make a rough sketch of the sweater to scale to determine where you want to position your motifs and embellishments, as shown in the drawing at far left. Don't be scared by the word sketch. A simple block drawing will be enough for you to proportion the design to the sweater size. Remember that when a child is wearing a sweater, the side seams are not visible; so although the sweater may be 16 in. wide across the front, you really have only about 12 in. of design space. I didn't make the stegosaurus the whole width of the sweater because his face and tail would have been hidden, which would diminish the effectiveness of the design.

Your sketch will give you a general idea of whether you need to simplify your design or add more details. In general, two good rules to follow are: Simplify the design, and exaggerate the details. Simple shapes with one or two very prominent details will intrigue a child. Look at your design idea and think of what your child would notice the most, then emphasize that detail. For example, the elephants in "Elephant Pyramid," shown on page 48 and at upper left, facing page, are very simple in shape—almost boxes with legs—but their ears are oversized and exaggerated. Another example is the "Rattler Sweater" (page 48 and at right). The snake's body is simply a very long strip in a slipped chevron stitch (directions at right), but his head is exaggerated with large "goo-goo" eyes and a red tongue. I wanted him to look like a rattler but not to be scary, so his exaggerated face adds a comical look.

There are many different ways to create the same motif. For example, a balloon could be knit in, appliquéd and stuffed, embroidered, or represented by a pom-pom or large button, whatever you like.   ⇨

Knit a snake

The "Rattler Sweater," page 49 and below, is knit with black, brown, and light brown sport-weight yarn and size six needles.

Tail—With light brown cast on 35 sts.
Rows 1 and 3: Knit.
Rows 2 and 4: Purl.
Rows 5 and 7: Purl.
Rows 6 and 8: Knit.
Row 9: Knit.
Row 10: Purl.
Repeat rows 5-10 three more times.
Work rows 5-8 one more time.
Bind off 4 sts beg of next 2 rows.

Body—Slipped chevron stitch. Change colors every 2 rows. Color sequence: black; lt. brown; lt. brown and brown, alternating 3 times; repeat.
• *M1:* (make 1) Lift running thread for a new st and knit into the back of it.
• *D3:* (vertical double decrease) Slip 2 tog knitwise, k1, pass 2 sl sts over.
• *Sl1:* Slip 1 st purlwise.
Row 1: k3, sl1, m1, k6, sl1, k1, D3, k1, sl1, k6, m1, sl1, k3.
Row 2: p12, sl1, p1, sl1, p12.
Row 3: k3, sl1, m1, k5, sl1, k2, D3, k2, sl1, k5, m1, sl1, k3.
Row 4: p11, sl1, p3, sl1, p11.
Row 5: k3, sl1, m1, k4, sl1, k3, D3, k3, sl1, k4, m1, sl1, k3.
Row 6: p10, sl1, p5, sl1, p10.
Row 7: k3, sl1, m1, k3, sl1, k4, D3, k4, sl1, k3, m1, sl1, k3.
Row 8: p9, sl1, p7, sl1, p9.
Row 9: k3, sl1, m1, k2, sl1, k5, D3, k5, sl1, k2, m1, sl1, k3.
Row 10: p8, sl1, p9, sl1, p8.
Row 11: k3, sl1, m1, kl, sl1, k6, D3, k6, sl1, k1, m1, sl1, k3.
Row 12: p7, sl1, p11, sl1, p7.
Row 13: k3, sl1, m1, sl1, k7, D3, k7, sl1, m1, sl1, k3.
Row 14: p6, sl1, p13, sl1, p6.
Repeat rows 1-14 until snake is 60 in. long or desired length for wrapping around sweater. Bind off.

Neck (underbelly)—With black yarn, cast on 27 sts. Work same pattern as for body, changing colors as described, until piece measures 5 in. Bind off.

Mouth—With black yarn, cast on 5 sts. Working in stockinette st, inc 1 st each side of center st, every other row until there are 27 sts. Work 4 rows even. Work D3 on center 3 sts, every other row until 5 sts remain. Bind off.

Finishing—Gather cast-on edge of tail and sew back seam. Insert rattle and whip stitch top of rattle pocket closed. At head end, fold under body and neck selvages along slip stitch edges, and sew neck to head (cast-on edge of neck is mouth end). Sew mouth into opening, and stuff head lightly. Attach large "goo-goo" eyes. Braid red tongue in mouth.
Wrap snake around sweater as desired. Sew to sweater along slip stitch edges, tucking color-change ends in (selvages will naturally roll under). Leave head and tail free. —W.K.

"Rattler" is embellished with a 5-ft. sewn-on snake. His tail, which hides a rattle, and his head are three-dimensional and move with the wearer.

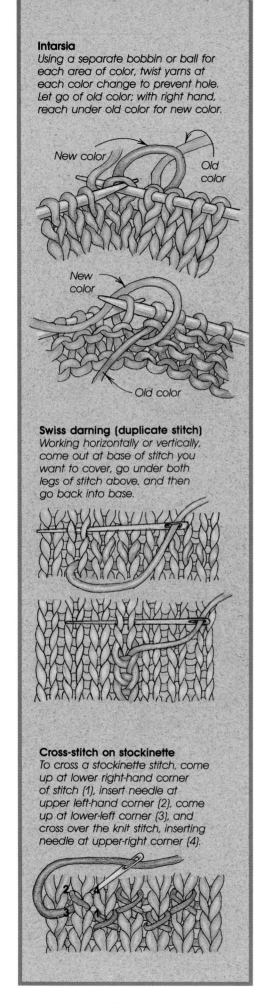

Intarsia
Using a separate bobbin or ball for each area of color, twist yarns at each color change to prevent hole. Let go of old color; with right hand, reach under old color for new color.

New color

Old color

New color

Old color

Swiss darning (duplicate stitch)
Working horizontally or vertically, come out at base of stitch you want to cover, go under both legs of stitch above, and then go back into base.

Cross-stitch on stockinette
To cross a stockinette stitch, come up at lower right-hand corner of stitch (1), insert needle at upper left-hand corner (2), come up at lower-left corner (3), and cross over the knit stitch, inserting needle at upper-right corner (4).

Knit-in designs—If you plan to use intarsia or swiss darning (duplicate stitch), shown at left, you need to graph the design. Using your sketch and gauge, determine approximately how many stitches and rows will be used in the whole piece and then in each motif. Next, using knitter's graph paper, block out a section the size of each motif, as shown on page 50. Don't use regular, square graph paper, or your design will look squashed when you knit it. Draw and refine your design in the blocked-out area on the graph paper without worrying about following the spaces. When it pleases you, fit the lines of your design to the stitch squares. The design won't look as blocky when you work it, so don't be upset by the jagged outlines.

Embellishing techniques—Your child's senses of sight and touch will be satisfied by these embellished sweaters, but also try to incorporate noisemakers to satisfy the sense of hearing. Jingle bells are widely available and fun. Squeakers and rattles are a little harder to find but well worth the effort (see Supplies at lower right). They are ideal for hiding under appliqués. Just for fun, don't tell your child you've hidden a squeaker under the appliquéd design and wait for the child's reaction when he or she finds it.

Keep in mind the age of your child and which embellishments are appropriate for that age. Beads, sequins, and "goo-goo" eyes are wonderful, but if your child is very young, use safer alternatives such as French knot eyes and embroidery. Many large, sturdy novelty buttons are also available, which I feel are suitable for any age child as long as you sew them on firmly. Squeakers and rattles can be a lot of fun for very young children; just be sure that the covering appliqué is sewn on securely.

Appliqué: Sew a shaped piece of knitting, fabric, etc., to the sweater. You can appliqué various materials to a sweater as long as cleaning and care are the same. For more dimension, lightly stuff appliqués with yarn scraps, polyester fiberfill, rattles, or squeakers.

Knitted flaps: Attach one side of small knitted pieces to the sweater fabric. Use increasing and decreasing along one or both edges to make the flaps any shape you desire. For example, the flag in "Elephant Pyramid" is decreased evenly along both edges to a single stitch, but the spines of the stegosaurus (knit in a continuous strip) are increased and then decreased along one edge only. Sew the flaps on at any angle or knit them in by working the flap stitches together with the sweater stitches at the place where you want them to attach. Use garter or seed stitch for flaps that you want to lie flat.

Embroidery: Many different embroidery stitches can be used on knitting. Some of the most commonly used and versatile include back stitch, chain stitch, stem stitch, couching, and French knots. Two books with good embroidery stitch instructions are listed below.

You can *cross-stitch* directly on a stockinette stitch fabric, using one cross-stitch for each knit stitch, as shown in the drawing at lower left, or you can cross-stitch on aida fabric and appliqué the cloth to the sweater. Using a fine aida fabric with 18 or 22 stitches per inch allows you to write messages on your sweater, as I did on the flag in "Elephant Pyramid."

The *Swiss darning or duplicate stitch* technique, shown at left center, allows you to cover plain stockinette completely, forming a motif over the knitting. The stitches will look slightly larger and somewhat raised as compared to the uncovered knit stitches. For large motifs, work swiss darning in blocks of stitches. Work from right to left to the end of the first row, turn the work upside down, and work the second row from right to left also.

Even though you've planned carefully, be flexible. As you work on the sweater, you may see opportunities to make simple changes. Remember, these sweaters derive their life and fun from embellishments, so don't be discouraged when your knitting is done and the sweater, even one with intarsia, looks plain. When you complete the embellishments, your planning will pay off, and the sweater will come to life.

Wendy Keele of Hastings, NE, is a free-lance knitwear designer.

Books

Enthoven, Jacqueline. *The Stitches of Creative Embroidery.* West Chester, PA: Schiffer Publishing, 1987.

Gibson-Roberts, Priscilla. *Knitting in the Old Way.* Loveland, CO: Interweave Press, 1985.

Snook, Barbara. *Embroidery Stitches.* New York: St. Martin's Press, 1986.

Zimmermann, Elizabeth. *Knitting Workshop.* Pittsville, WI: Schoolhouse Press, 1984.

Supplies

Aardvark Adventures
Box 2449
Livermore, CA 94551-0241
Squeakers and rattles; sample issue, $2; minimum order, $15.

Schoolhouse Press
6899 Cary Bluff
Pittsville, WI 54466
(715) 884-2799
Knitter's graph paper; $2 for wool samples, booklist, and unusual knitting tools.

Comforting Sweaters Wrap You in a Picture

Easy embroidery stitches add definition to simple blocks of color

by Judith Swartz

"**d**on't forget to take a sweater," the motherly advice that always followed me out the door as a child, taught me that a sweater holds an important place as a garment. Because I associate sweaters with security and warmth, much of the imagery in my work expresses warmth and contentment, with an element of humor. I often depict interior, homey themes; certain symbols, such as dogs and overstuffed armchairs, which always evoke a positive response from me reappear from sweater to sweater (photo on p. 57). As complex as my images seem to be, they are actually easy to knit. The sweater shapes are simple cardigans. Instead of trying to integrate all the color in the knitting, I design with large blocks of color. What look like thin lines and difficult dots of intarsia are actually just surface embroidery.

You can design a garment as a painting, then wear it as a sculpture as I do. Envision the sweater as a large rectangle, like a canvas. My technique involves using color like a painter, first drawing, then knitting large areas of color with small patches of yarn, then working back into those knitted areas with embroidery to build up richness, shading, and detail.

When the flat image wraps around a body (see the drawing at right) and echoes the body shape, it becomes a sculpture. Ironically, such images are never seen as a whole. I create designs that flow together as a whole but also present changed images from front to back, drawing the viewers' eyes around the garment and surprising them along the way.

Designing a sweater as a rectangle

Decide on a shape for your garment first. My goal is to create timeless garments, so I choose a classic shape and a generous fit. A simple silhouette, usually a V-neck cardigan, works well, so that the shape does not detract from the subject.

Now, in your mind, remove the sleeves from this simple shape and unfold the fronts so that you have a large rectangular canvas on which to design. In this way, you can plan the image for the entire sweater at one time. Your inspiration may come from personal thoughts or experiences, or from other sources such as a painting, photograph, nature, ethnic inspiration, political statement, or cartoon. Having a source to work from is a good exercise in design and decision making. You don't want to copy the source, but to abstract from it and make it personal. Starting to think of colors and yarn textures will make the ideas more concrete.

Translating a design concept into a pattern and from that into an actual gar-

Judith Swartz lives with her cat named Charlotte Isabel Purrkins in Chicago, IL, where Judith designs and produces knitwear and teaches classes in creating sweaters at the Textile Arts Centre.

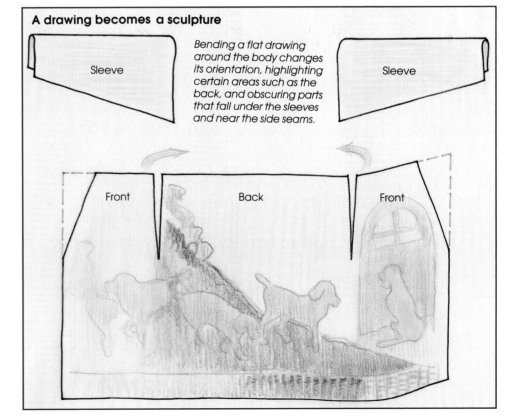

A drawing becomes a sculpture

Bending a flat drawing around the body changes its orientation, highlighting certain areas such as the back, and obscuring parts that fall under the sleeves and near the side seams.

Sleeve

Sleeve

Front

Back

Front

Simple embroidery stitches enhance knits

Try my embroidery techniques to embellish a new or old knitted garment. You can add details to intarsia, as I do, or transform a perfectly plain (and perhaps boring) sweater into something entirely different.

Although I embroider my knitted garments heavily, I use only a few simple embroidery stitches, such as the chain stitch, duplicate stitch (see the drawings on the facing page), running stitch, and occasionally, French knots. There are two reasons for keeping the embroidery simple.

First, when knitted fabric is embroidered, it tends to distort easily and won't remain taut in a hoop, which would be necessary for more complex stitches.

Second, the function of the embroidery is to enhance the knitted surface, rather than become a focal point. Ideally, the finished surface is so well integrated that the viewer sees both elements as one and cannot immediately distinguish where the knitting leaves off and the embroidery begins.

I work most of the embroidery before assembling the garment, because smaller pieces are easier to handle. Placing each sweater section flat on a table while I stitch, I check frequently to ensure that the embroidery stitches aren't distorting the shape. I save the lines of embroidery that cross a seam to complete after the seam is sewn.

I prefer chain stitch and duplicate stitch because they most closely resemble knitting stitches. Chain stitch works well for outlining shapes and adding details, such as the dividers between panes in a window (as in the left-hand sweater shown in the photo on p. 57). After much trial and error, I have found chain stitch easier to control on the knitted surface than a traditional outline stitch, which uses a backstitch and tends to be inconsistent, especially on curves. In order to keep embroidery tension even, use the knitted surface as a guide, matching one chain stitch to each knit stitch. If you're working the chain stitch in a lighter-weight yarn, such as pearl cotton, on a heavy wool (as in the "Letting the Dogs In and Out" sweater in the photo on p. 56), embroider two chain stitches for each knit stitch.

Duplicate stitch is best for areas where just a few stitches of detail are desired. In the sweater "Seals in a Snowstorm" (see facing page), I used duplicate stitch for the snowflakes, the zigzag pattern on the front, sleeve, and hem bands, and for shading the landscape and ice floes. If you use too many stitches in one area, the surface becomes more dense and the work distorts. I sometimes shade an area by duplicate stitching every other stitch for a halftone effect, as in the intersections of the three red yarns (bright red in the center, soft red on bottom, deep red along the edge) on the back of the sweater on p. 56.

For just a hint of color, I use a running stitch or half a duplicate stitch. The lighter flakes of snow in "Seals in a Snowstorm" on the facing page consist of half-duplicate stitches, and the seals' whiskers are worked in small running stitches in a finer, shiny rayon yarn. French knots work well when I want small amounts of both color and texture.

Use chain stitch in a similar shade to add texture, or combine stitches in one or more contrasting colors to build an interesting design in geometric shapes, curves, or realistic images. —J.S.

Chain-stitch embroidery, worked flat on the garment sections before assembly, echoes the shape of a knitted stitch. This technique allows the embroidered details to blend right into the knitted background for a smooth, unified effect.

ment requires several considerations. You are designing for a human form, so what might look wonderful on paper will change when it is draped on the body, with different areas of the design being highlighted and obscured. Parts of the image that fall under the arm or close to the side seams tend to disappear. Continue the design through these areas, but avoid placing the most important elements where they will not be seen, or you risk losing the integrity of the design.

In women's garments, pay attention to the bustline, placing major areas of design or color either above or below. More often than not, the strongest statement I make is on the back of a garment. The back provides the smoothest, largest surface of the garment and does not detract from or compete with the wearer's face. I enjoy the surprise element of having the focal point on the back, and I use it as an opportunity to lead the viewer around the garment as the image unfolds.

One of the challenges of designing an art garment is to integrate the separate areas of the body, sleeves, and possibly a collar. Ideally, these separate pieces either come together as a whole idea, with the design flowing throughout the garment as a single statement, or they play against one another, creating a harmonious balance.

Sleeves often present a difficult design problem, for several reasons. First, when the garment is worn the sleeve moves the most: The orientation of the image constantly changes as an arm moves up to fluff the hair, straightens out to ring a doorbell, then hangs down at the side of the body. Second, there is a rather narrow area of the sleeve where the image is clearly visible. If this is not a continuation of the main image, take care that it does not overpower or fight with the main image. One option is to repeat or abstract an image from the main design. This motif may be repeated over the entire sleeve or placed as a single motif. Sometimes the sleeve image can be a suggestion of the whole. For example, with an interior scene, the sleeves will often contain just a window or a doorway. In the sweaters shown in the photo on p. 57, the seal sweater sleeves continue the sky and snow from the body, while the dog sweater sleeves repeat smaller images of "letting the dogs out": they appear to be escaping through slits in the sleeve itself (see the photo on p. 56).

Stitches for decorating knits

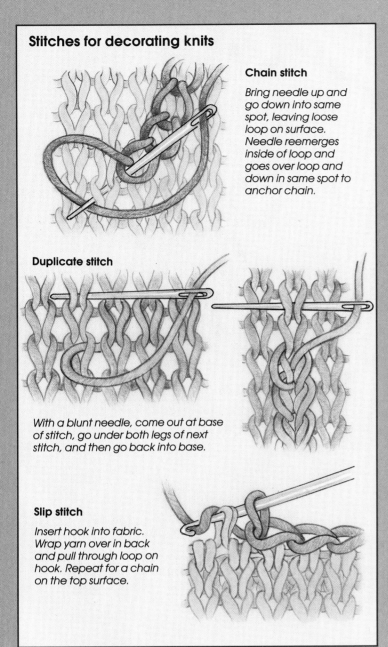

Chain stitch

Bring needle up and go down into same spot, leaving loose loop on surface. Needle reemerges inside of loop and goes over loop and down in same spot to anchor chain.

Duplicate stitch

With a blunt needle, come out at base of stitch, go under both legs of next stitch, and then go back into base.

Slip stitch

Insert hook into fabric. Wrap yarn over in back and pull through loop on hook. Repeat for a chain on the top surface.

Duplicate stitch and half-duplicate stitch form the snowflakes and shading. Slip-stitch crochet alternating with loops of crocheted chains make the asymmetrical buttonholes.

After you sketch the design and choose a silhouette, the next step is to create a schematic drawing. This is simply an outline of each piece, noting all the dimensions. The written pattern and the pattern graph will be created from the schematic drawing and gauge swatches.

Working with yarns and swatches

When choosing yarns, try to stay within the same gauge range. Make a separate gauge swatch at least 4 in. square for each yarn you plan to use, to make sure the gauges match. If you can't obtain similar gauges for contrasting yarns, adjust by adding a second strand to thinner yarns, and consider eliminating yarns that are too thick. Using a contrasting yarn with a slightly different gauge in only a small area should not cause a problem.

When mixing different fibers in a piece, such as a wool and a rayon yarn of similar gauges, maintain a balance between the fibers. Wool yarn tends to be buoyant and springy, while rayon yarn drapes and falls. Interspersing these two yarns evenly throughout will result in a balanced fabric. But if the wool and rayon yarns are used alone in large sections, those sections will behave differently. Gravity will exaggerate the effect and detract from the finished garment.

Developing the pattern graph

Calculate the pattern using the gauge of the main yarn, carefully measuring the stitch and the row gauge to create an accurate graph. I recommend using a calculator and including fractions. To determine the correct number of stitches and rows for a piece, multiply the width of the piece by the stitch gauge, and the length of the piece by the row gauge. Calculate the number of stitches and rows for each section of your garment.

After you calculate the pattern, transfer it to knitters' graph paper, which is essential to maintain the proportions of the knit stitch (more rows per inch than stitches per inch). While knitters' graph paper is available in a variety of gauges, don't worry about matching your stitch gauge, as the proportion remains relatively the same. Make sure that you have a large enough piece of paper to accommodate the total number of stitches and rows in a pattern piece; you may have to tape several pieces of paper together.

To transfer your design and pattern to the graph paper, the first step is to out-

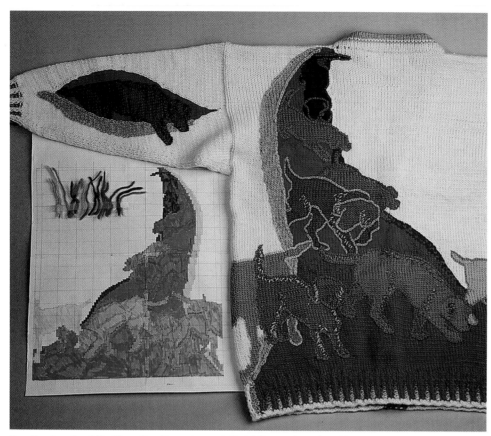

For the back of "Letting the Dogs In and Out," the colored pattern graph at left acts as a map for the simple intarsia knitting, whether worked by hand or machine. Note that this machine-knitted example reverses the image of the chart.

line the perimeter of each piece. There are no shortcuts here but to simply count out the squares. Each square represents a stitch. Once you have the outline, draw your design lightly in pencil directly on the graph paper. If your design is one that flows from piece to piece, temporarily tape the pieces together for matching purposes, and mark where the sleeves will meet the body to help in design placement decisions. When the design is completely drawn, go back over the lines with a bolder pencil, translating them into stitches by outlining the squares that most closely approximate the lines. The final step in graph preparation is adding color. I recommend colored pencils as you can still see the graph through them. Not only does coloring allow you to test color placement, but it makes the graph much easier to follow while knitting (see the photo above). Your graph should contain as much detail as you are certain of at this point, even if many of the details will be embroidered later. It is much easier to have all the information contained in one reference. For further ease and accuracy, pencil every ten stitches and rows in a grid superimposed over the graph. Then, while knitting, highlight every ten rows with a transparent marker to mark your progress.

Knitting the sections

Whether working by hand or machine intarsia, you are now ready to begin knitting. (See the article on p. 69 for helpful intarsia techniques.) If you use a knitting machine, remember that your image will appear as the reverse of your graph, because, on most machines, the purl side of the work faces you.

Effective edge treatments contain the garment's images, either as a frame in a contrasting color, or as a unifying element incorporating the colors of the image. Whether you choose to hand- or machine knit a traditional ribbing or a nontraditional edge such as a roll or a flat double hem, the edge should complement the garment's image. Both sweaters in the photo on p. 57 have edgings that repeat the colors of the image, the one on the right with flat hems, the other with handknitted ribbing. I like to use this multicolored ribbing borrowed from a Scandinavian sweater. On the right side, the knit stitches remain one color, and the purl stitches are in stripes, changing every two or three rows. This technique draws colors in more subtly than conventional horizontal striping, as the color change occurs only in the purl stitches. For this finish, machine knit the garment sections first, beginning each sec-

tion with a few rows of waste yarn (see *Basics, Threads* No. 44). When your are ready to handknit the ribbings, unravel the waste rows, pick up the stitches, and knit down, taking care not to cast off too tightly.

Sometimes I knit a special facing inside the neck and front bands, such as bright stripes or a pattern, as a treat to be known to the wearer but not to the viewer. This secret detail imparts a special feeling.

If the image requires no framing, a row or two of single crochet stabilizes the edge and helps to prevent curling. Or one of the interesting crochet stitches specifically for edges can add a decorative element. Try the crab stitch, or backward crochet (see *Basics, Threads* No. 44), which makes an attractive corded edge.

Cleaning up

Knitting by machine distorts and stiffens the work, so I steam and measure the first piece off the machine to check the accuracy of my gauge and to make the fabric more pliable. After knitting, steam each piece, then weave in the numerous ends created by intarsia, which is essential for the structural integrity of the fabric. If handknitting, you may be able to incorporate some of these ends while knitting, but with machine intarsia, I clean up the ends afterwards. Use a blunt tapestry needle to weave in ends and close up any small spaces between colors that may have occurred during knitting. To keep ends from popping through to the right side, leave a little longer tail when trimming worked-in ends, especially when knitting with cotton and other smooth yarns that do not cling to each other, as wool does.

For smooth, asymmetrical buttonholes, I often crochet a slip stitch (see the drawing on p. 55) along the edge of the right front band (for a woman's sweater), working four or five crochet chain stitches (and skipping three band stitches) where I want each button loop. Sew the buttons on the inner edge of the opposite band.

After cleaning up the loose ends, most of the embroidery can be done in pieces (see instructions on p. 54), before assembling the sweater. Embroider as though you were painting, adding as much embellishment as necessary to bring out the design and balance the composition. As in painting, take time to step back for a critical view. □

Wrapping the wearer in images of warmth and contentment, the sweaters on the facing page combine knitting with simple embroidery embellishment. The embroidery blends with the knitting to create a smooth result that looks complex, but isn't.

Photo by Susan Kahn

When you understand how the two elements of knit lace work, yarnovers and decreases, you can chart your own free-form designs, as Alice Starmore did in her "Flying Birds" pullover. (Photo this page by Yvonne Taylor; photos pp. 59-63 by Susan Kahn)

Charting Lace
Work visually: knitted lace is easy to design

by Alice Starmore

ewcomers to the art of knitted lace are amazed to discover that the techniques are remarkably few and simple, with only two basic elements: Yarnovers make the holes, but they also create new stitches; decreases compensate for those new stitches (see *Basics, Threads* No. 32). (To make a yarnover, you simply bring the yarn over the right-hand needle without knitting a stitch from the left needle. The effect is a new stitch.) The arrangement of yarnovers and decreases forms the pattern.

The established way of providing instructions is to write them row by row. But written instructions do not convey any sense of what the pattern looks like. The problem is compounded with lace instructions, because a pattern of anything but the simplest form is an eye-boggling chunk of repeated letters and numbers in which it is all too easy to become hopelessly lost. Sound familiar?

The obvious and easy alternative is to use pictures instead of words. Charted lace patterns give a clear, visual explanation, using symbols that actually look like the stitches. They are easy to follow while working along each row, and each stitch and row can be seen and checked in relation to those above, below, and alongside. But by far the most exciting aspect of charted lace is that it makes the designing of your own original lace patterns not only possible, but easy and a lot of fun. It is with this goal in mind that I have planned the following series of pattern exercises.

Reading charts

First, it is vital to learn how to read and work from a chart. To do this, have a look at Chart 1—"Eyelets," and the knitted sample below it as I explain how it works. The chart represents a swatch of knitting placed right side up, with the cast-on edge at the bottom. Each square represents a stitch and contains a symbol which conveys an instruction. The × in the square at each side represents a selvage stitch, which is extra to the lace pattern. It may be

worked simply as a garter stitch or as a more elaborate edge such as a picot selvage (see *Threads* No. 23, pp. 44-45). The Ⅰ symbolizes a knit stitch, which has a vertical appearance on the right side. The ○ is for the yarnover (yo), which produces a hole. And the final symbol on this chart is the ∧ for knit 2 stitches together (k2tog). When a k2tog is worked, the second stitch slants to the right and covers the top of the first stitch, so the symbol appears as two lines (the two stitches) with the second line slanting to the right to meet the top of the first. This gives you a clear picture of what "Eyelets" will look like—a solid fabric punctuated by single holes spaced at regular intervals (photo, right). We'll talk about designing with both right- and left-slanting decreases shortly.

Each horizontal row of squares represents a row of knitting and is read just as the knitting is worked: The first row (right side) is at the bottom and is worked from right to left. Wrong-side rows are even numbers, and are worked from left to right. Only the right-side rows are shown on the chart because in this pattern, as in many other lace patterns, the wrong-side rows are purled straight across all pattern stitches, so it is not necessary to chart them. Also, omitting plain wrong-side rows actually gives a better picture of the pattern on the chart because lace knitting does not have a square gauge. There are more rows than stitches to a given measurement, and the holes are larger and the decreases more prominent than the rows of plain stitches. After working the last charted row at the top, you must work a wrong-side row before starting again from row 1.

The pattern repeat is outlined in the chart. The stitches at each side of the repeat center the pattern across the row, and the minimum swatch size will contain exactly the number of stitches shown in one horizontal row of the chart. To make a larger piece, add multiples of the stitch repeat. In other words, cast on the multiple, as many times as desired, plus the total number of stitches at each side.

Now that you understand how to read and

From *Threads* magazine (December 1990) 32:68-73

Key to symbols

⊠ Selvage   Ⅰ Knit   ○ Yarnover (yo)
◿ Knit 2 together (k2tog) (right-slanting)
◺ Slip, slip, knit together (ssk) (left-slanting)
◹ Slip 1-knit 2 tog-pass sl st over (sl 1-k2tog-psso)
Blue outlines indicate pattern and row repeat

1. Eyelets

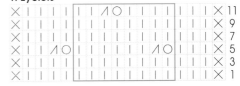

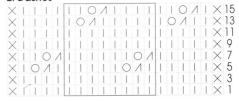

The decrease slants toward the hole, minimizing the slant.

2. Dashes

The decrease slants away from the hole, accentuating the slant.

3. Little Parallelograms

4a. Squares, slanting right

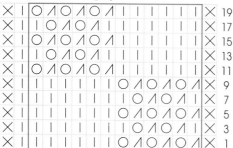

4b. Squares, slanting left

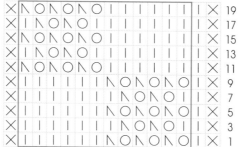

4c. Squares, with a fault

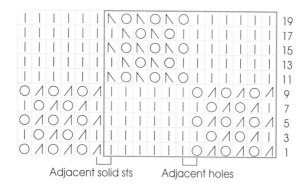

Adjacent solid sts   Adjacent holes

The smart way to design
4d. Squares, slanting right and left

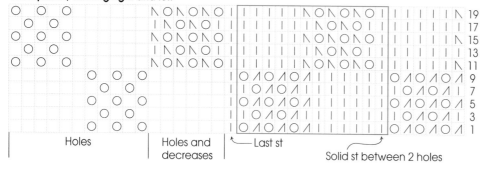

Holes   Holes and   Last st
               decreases
                              Solid st between 2 holes

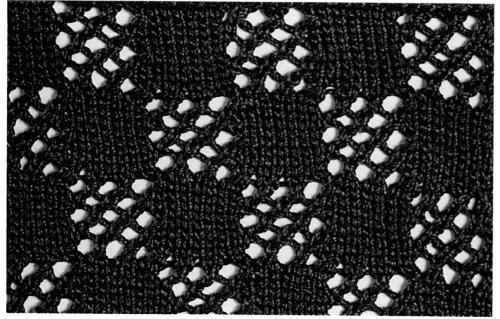

In charting lace, learn to think in terms of just two elements: holes and solid stitches. The photo above is "Squares" (chart 4a). The k2tog decreases accentuate the rightward slant of the holes.

work from a chart, you are ready to study charts from a design point of view. Have a look at "Eyelets" again. Already you can see how simple it would be to chart a variation of this pattern by simply moving the yo/decrease pairs closer together or further apart to make a larger or smaller pattern.

The effect of slanting decreases

The appearance of the hole is affected by where you place the decrease. Looking at the k2tog decrease on Chart 1, you can see how it will look in the knitted piece: The right slant is slightly discernible, and the hole is to its right on the vertical side. You can accentuate the slant if you plot the yo at the immediate left of the decrease, instead of at the immediate right (see Chart 2, p. 59). It will show up sharper because the slanted side of the stitch is followed by the hole rather than by a solid stitch.

Chart 2—"Dashes," center, p. 59, is a simple pattern resulting from the idea of accentuating the slant by plotting a k2tog, yo, and then another k2tog, yo, one stitch to the right on the next right-side row.

Chart 3—"Little Parallelograms," at bottom, p. 59, is a direct follow-through from "Dashes." It expands the k2tog, yo over four stitches and three right-side rows, arranging them with the same number of solid stitches between. Although the pattern can be viewed completely after row 11, it is necessary to chart the 23 rows in order to begin the row repeat at the correct position.

Another important consideration is bias. If the k2tog decreases and yos cover an entire pattern, the resulting fabric will bias to the right. This is even more extreme when they are placed one directly above the other. In chart 3, the areas of stockinette render any tendency for bias so slight as to be unnoticeable and easily corrected with blocking.

Chart 4a—"Squares," at far upper left, continues the theme of simple geometric shapes with the sharp diagonals of the decreases adding an interesting slant. In order to produce a square shape, each lace square occupies six stitches and ten rows.

Chart 4b (near upper left) is the same "Squares" pattern but the decreases slant to the left and *follow* the yarnovers. This accentuates the leftward slant. ⋀ is the symbol for the slip, slip, knit decrease (ssk—slip two sts one at a time knitwise, then knit them together); it is the counterpart of k2tog, having the same degree of slant in the opposite direction. Note that the stockinette stitch outside the repeat is on the right rather than on the left, as it is in 4a. Since the position of the decreases has been reversed, the extra stitch must also be reversed so that the holes in each band of squares are equidistant from the selvages.

My next idea was to make a "Squares"

pattern with alternating bands of right- and left-slanting decreases. You might think that the obvious thing to do is to plot a pattern repeat of rows 1 through 9 of 4a, followed by rows 11 through 19 of 4b, which I charted in 4c (center, facing page). At first glance, this looks fine, with the upper lace square plotted exactly in the space between the two below. But if you knit this pattern, the lace square above appears much closer to the square below right than to the square below left. This is because the corner holes are adjacent to each other on the right, but there are two solid stitches between them on the left.

This kind of fault arises through including the outer decreases as part of the lace squares. Although, technically, they are, the holes are the prominent feature. The decreases affect the pattern, but it is important to realize that solid stitches next to other solid stitches are not that noticeable.

The intelligent way to design

Another important reason why Chart 4c doesn't work is because I took the wrong approach in designing it—charting it line for line from the previous two charts. Just as it would be ridiculous to paint a picture starting at the corner and painting in horizontal lines, so it is with lace patterns.

The right approach is shown in Chart 4d (lower chart, facing page): Begin by plotting the main feature of the pattern, which is usually the holes (the yos, on the left-hand side of the chart). Work on a large piece of graph paper plotting the yos and covering a fairly large area, especially widthways. The next step is to plot the decreases, making sure to have a decrease for each yo. Notice that between each square of holes, I have left only one vertical space for a solid stitch. On the first nine rows, a decrease precedes each hole; on rows 11-19, a decrease follows each hole. Next, plot the symbols for the solid stitches. Now you can study the pattern and work out the stitch repeat. Outline the repeat and then outline any stitches to be worked at each side so that the pattern is centered. Before knitting, you should rechart the outlined pattern, add the selvage stitches, and number the rows.

Looking at the outlined pattern, 4d, notice that the two squares of holes now have one solid stitch running up between them on each side. On one side, the solid stitch has a decrease on alternate rows. It knits up as a slight ridge but does not unbalance or distract from the pattern.

Chart 5a, "Diagonal Diamonds," above right, is a direct progression from "Squares," but it is a little more sophisticated. The layout of the left- and right-slanted diamonds means that there are both k2tog and ssk decreases in most rows. It was very important

Knitting from your charts is the acid test. The "Diagonal Diamonds" (chart 5b) are evenly spaced.

5a. Diagonal Diamonds
The outline marks a repeat plus two sts on the left to center the pattern.

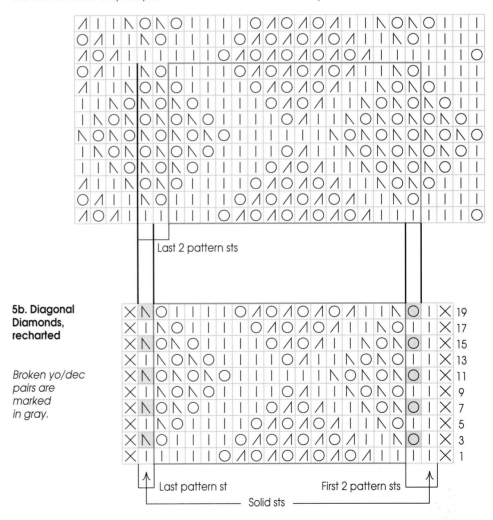

Last 2 pattern sts

5b. Diagonal Diamonds, recharted

Broken yo/dec pairs are marked in gray.

Last pattern st   First 2 pattern sts

Solid sts

The multiple has been moved one st to the left, and the extra, centering, pattern sts complete broken pairs. Plain sts fill in unbroken pairs.

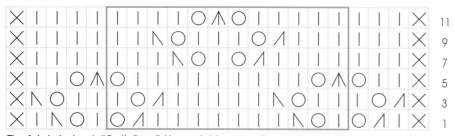

The fabric below is "Cat's Paw." Above right you see the expanded "Cat's Paw Diamond" with "Vertical Cat's Paws" on either side.

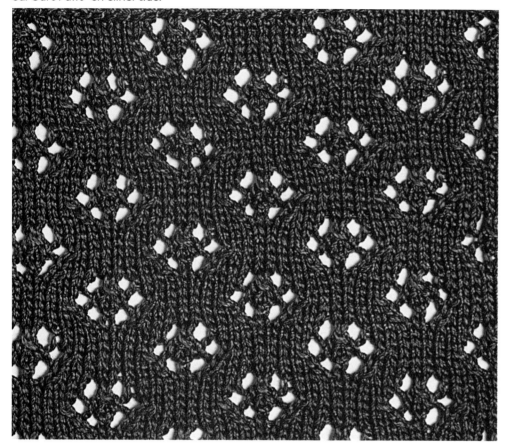

7. Vertical Cat's Paw

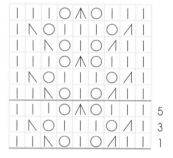

8. Cat's Paw Diamond

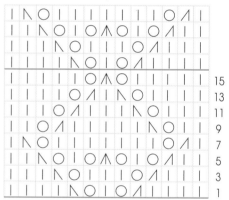

for me to rechart the outlined stitches because I had to make some changes in order to knit the pattern successfully. For one thing, no matter where you draw the repeat outline, the diamonds that get split on each side of the knitted piece will have either a decrease or a yo extra. In the case of 5a, the diamond that is split at the right of the outline has one too many decreases on every alternate row, while on the left side it has one too many yos.

Chart 5b shows the pattern recharted correctly. I have moved the repeat to the left one stitch to split the diamond exactly in half, put stitches on each side to center and take care of the extra decs on right and extra yos on left, and added a plain stitch on the right to center the holes perfectly.

When you have outlined the repeat and the stitches that center the pattern, always check that each yo has a corresponding decrease, and vice versa; it may be necessary to make adjustments like this when you rechart for knitting.

Designing with paired decreases

Now we're ready to explore the classic idea of paired decreases, the basis of innumerable patterns and the platform from which to take off on your own flights of fancy. The principle is simplicity itself. Have a look at Chart 6–"Cat's Paws," above. This simple Shetland lace motif is a perfect key to understanding the essence of knitted lace design. The base, or first row, of each motif is crucial. As you can see, it is composed of a central solid stitch, on either side of which is a yarnover and a decrease. The right-slanting decrease on the right is reflected exactly by the left-slanting decrease on the left to produce perfect symmetry. On the next right-side row, the motif is opened out with three central solid stitches and reflecting yo/decreases at each side. The motif is then closed by working a central double decrease, which gathers three sts into one (sl 1-k2tog-psso, see *Basics, Threads* No. 32), shown on the chart by the ⋀. A yarnover at each side compensates symmetrically for the two stitches reduced by the double decrease. The important points to note are the symmetrical placing of the yarnovers and decreases, and the typical first row, which you can use as the opening for all kinds of patterns. The degree of elaboration on this theme is entirely up to you.

A fascinating part of the designing process is arranging motifs into a design. The next two charts, above, show the results of a small experiment in arranging the Cat's Paw motif and elaborating on it. Chart 7 has the motifs arranged directly above each other in a vertical panel. There are just six rows (including the last purl row) per repeat, although I have shown more so that you can see how it looks. The effect is quite different from the original. In Chart 8—"Cat's Paw Diamond" (facing page), I elaborated on the original motif by continuing it into a larger diamond form. You can work the diamonds in Charts 7 and 8 side by side in a vertical panel arrangement with plain stockinette between each panel, as shown in the photograph at upper right, facing page, or with a wide variety of open or solid stitches between. When you experiment, you will find that one idea will follow another and that you can create many variations on a single pattern.

Designing your own lace images

Up to this point I have worked with such small motifs and basic arrangements that I would be very surprised if any of the designs were new inventions. But it is possible to work within a simple geometric framework and create endless new designs by elaborating on basic arrangements. You can also work with irregular shapes. For example, nature provides many beautiful forms that can inspire lace designs, such as my "Butterfly," shown at lower right.

I visualized the butterfly's wings as lacy and delicate and the body as a solid contrast. With that in mind, I plotted out the holes first and then added the decreases, as shown in Chart 9, at right. I accentuated the butterfly's vertical line of symmetry by using reflecting decreases on each side. To differentiate the top and bottom pair of wings, I made the diagonals point outward on the top pair and inward on the bottom pair. The paired decreases encroach on the body space, but this is fine as they are solid stitches like the body and will be seen as part of it.

On the tail end I plotted a single hole at the bottom, and the decrease is a k2tog *following* the yo, thus softening the slant of the decrease and diminishing the effect of its asymmetry. I thought the tail would look further separated from the wings with double decreases in the center, rather than single ones at each side. Of course, the decrease where the tail meets the body had to be a double, because there was already a yarnover at each side. I used double decreases for the head for the same reason. The decreases at the tips of the antennae are not accentuated because I wanted them to point ahead. If I had plotted the decreases as the ones directly below, they would have pointed outwards a little too much. Once the motif was charted to satisfaction, the next step was to knit a swatch to see that it worked as planned. □

Alice Starmore, who lives on the Isle of Lewis in Scotland, is a frequent contributor to Threads.

9. Butterfly

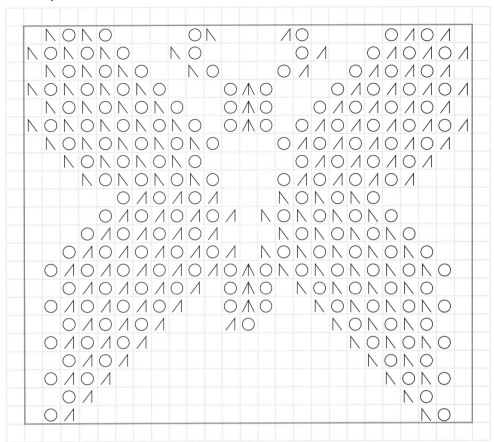

The butterfly chart is the centerpiece of Starmore's curtain. She used paired decreases and cat's paw variations to design the other elements.

Knitting a Patchwork of Patterns

Balancing tension is the key to mixing many textures in the same sweater

by Sally Melville

texture in knitting has always fascinated me. Most of the intricate, sculptural fabrics you can produce simply by crossing some stitches over others, by building up small areas as bobbles, or by leaving holes for lace are impossible to make with other techniques—at least in such plentitude. And although color knitting has been very popular for years, I've felt it would be a shame if the new approaches to color continued to capture *all* the attention. I asked myself how I could use stitch patterns to generate the excitement and attention that texture deserves.

I began my exploration in a most unlikely situation: on a bus chaperoning 50 eighth-graders. Perhaps their energy and enthusiasm stimulated me. Or perhaps I needed a project so exciting and complex that the concentration required would force out the noise and activity around me.

I considered Arans, horizontal stripes, asymmetrical vertical stripes (you can see the result on p. 68), and a sewn-together patchwork. My vertical stripe approach to asymmetrical texture design is a good place to start playing with complex textures. But I wanted something even more intricate and exciting looking. A final option, which I found irresistible, was to work each garment piece with constant change of texture. In the cream-colored pullover shown on the facing page, I changed stitch patterns often, both horizontally and vertically, without regularity or symmetry. Because I used many stitch patterns at once, I knit few intricate ones at the same time. But the many erratic changes in texture produced an exciting complexity automatically—the look I had been searching for!

The only real problem with combining varied texture patterns is that they may have incompatible tensions. So I'll explain how you make stitch-count adjustments to accommodate for this. I'll also explain how to choose appropriate patterns, color, yarn, and garment shape and how to lay out a design.

Appropriate stitch patterns

All approaches to combining patterns have one essential problem: Different stitch patterns produce different sts/in. tensions with the same yarn and the same size needles. To see just how varied these tensions are, look at the swatches on p. 67. That peculiar hourglass shape would cause problems in a garment. Different stitch patterns may also produce different rows/in. tensions, but I've found that gravity helps the garment accommodate this difference, so I don't worry about it.

Start by trying out familiar patterns in a sampler scarf, one after another. Only if the sides remain straight are the tensions compatible. Also, if some patterns recede too much, as stockinette stitch does, or bulge too much, as does reverse stockinette stitch, they are not aesthetically compatible; the work looks best if the patterns lie in the same plane. Checking your patterns this way is also a good idea because it helps familiarize you with them, so they'll be easier to knit.

You may also need to borrow from stitch dictionaries. I've provided some basic guidelines to help you choose patterns that work well together. The letters that precede the patterns below are keyed to the schematic on p. 66 so you can see where I placed various pattern types.

A. Balanced knit and purl patterns— Look for patterns that use knit and purl on the right side in more or less equal combination, over relatively limited areas each, and such that they constantly offset each other. For example:

• *Moss or seed stitch* is an equal combination (k to p) in a limited area of only one stitch of each, offset (otherwise, it would be k1, p1 rib).

• *2x2 Moss* (box stitch—k2, p2) is similar.

• *Garter stitch* (knit every row) alternates one row of stockinette with one row of reverse stockinette.

If you find a pattern you like that doesn't follow the guidelines, usually because it has too much stockinette (knit RS, purl WS) or reverse stockinette (purl RS, knit WS), try replacing some of it with moss or garter.

B. Rib patterns—Although ribbing is the most basic of knit and purl patterns, it obviously doesn't follow the guidelines because the knits and purls aren't offset. You can use many rib patterns, however, as long as you interrupt them every two rows with two rows of garter.

C. Lace patterns—While lace usually involves large areas of stockinette and so doesn't follow the knit/purl guidelines, the holes in the lace actually make the area lie flat and adjust to other tensions. So go ahead and try lace, particularly patterns with some texture (moss or garter) that will be aesthetically compatible with the knit/purl patterns.

D. Slipped- and dropped-stitch patterns—Unusual tensions generally make these incompatible with other patterns. But each is an individual case that you should try before discarding.

E. Bobble patterns—Bobbles, which are so textural (see the photos on p. 68), are instantly rewarding. Look for those that

From *Threads* magazine (October 1992) 43:50-54

follow the knit and purl guidelines or that need only minor adjustments. You can also work out your own arrangement of bobbles easily. On the right shoulder of my cream-colored sweater (schematic on p. 66), I placed them at regular intervals in the middle of a right-side k1, p5 (p3 also works), k1 vertical column. On the horizontal bands, the bobbles are evenly spaced in the middle, right-side row of a three-row stripe of reverse stockinette.

F. Cables—Cables add the most texture. But they also pose the greatest problem of incompatible tension because crossing the stitches narrows the width of the fabric significantly, as you can see from the hourglass shape on the samplers on p. 67. Tension adjustments, described below, will prevent this.

Tension adjustments

When a pattern has a markedly different tension from the ones below and above it, you need to add or remove stitches to accommodate it.

For cables—After a cable has been crossed, three or four stitches are really only the width of two or three plain stitches. So when you plan to use a cable, make a tension adjustment by allowing it only two-thirds or three-quarters of the number of stitches it actually requires. You add the missing stitches just before they are really needed, increasing on the row before the first cross. Immediately crossing the stitches hides the increases that keep the width constant. The added stitches stay in the cable pattern until the row after the final cross, where you decrease in preparation for the next pattern.

For example, for a cable pattern that requires 12 stitches, start with only 9 stitches (¾ of 12). If the first row of the pattern reads k4, p4, k4, work it k3, p3, k3. On the row before the first cross (usually the wrong side), increase one stitch in each set of three. The next row now has 12 stitches and is ready to be crossed. For the duration of this pattern, you will have 12 stitches. On the row after the final cross (usually the wrong side), decrease one stitch in each set of four, so the next row is back to the original nine and you're ready to begin a new pattern.

I work with either ¾ or ⅔ of the total stitch count, depending on which works better for any given cable pattern. This is determined by how many stitches are actually involved in the crossings. If you are crossing multiples of four, use ¾; if crossing multiples of three, use ⅔. To see how many stitches are crossed, examine the cable pattern. Do all the stitches

Random and irregularly sized blocks of textured stitch patterns form a dynamic design when knit together. You'll learn how to select patterns, allow for different tensions, and draw a schematic with all the patterns knit in one piece. (Photo by Yvonne Taylor)

Schematic design for back of pullover (medium)

Draw large schematic for each sweater piece. Mark lengths in inches and widths in inches and sts. Place most complex patterns first (C-F) to allow them adequate space and pride of place. Fill in with smaller areas of simpler patterns and vertical outlines (A-B).

Mark each space with number of sts—according to stockinette gauge (here let 6 sts = 1 in.)—and indicate sts to add and subtract for adjustments in cable and other non-gauge patterns.

Colored letters refer to pattern type, numbers to specific patterns, referenced at right. Similar patterns from other stitch dictionaries can be substituted. Patterns 13 and 14 were designed by the author, directions in "Original patterns" at right.

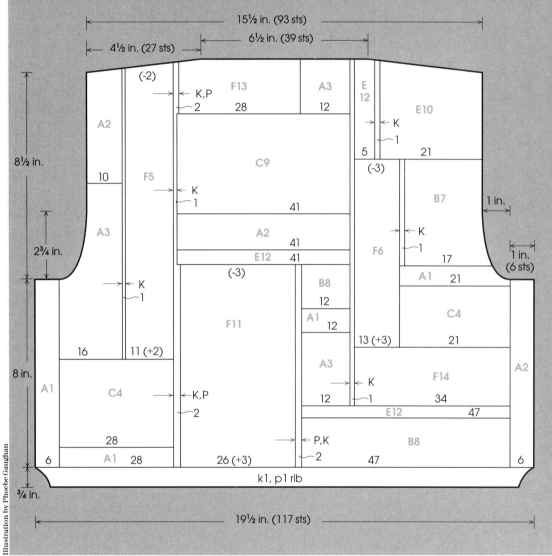

Illustration by Phoebe Gaughan

Original patterns
Key to abbreviations

C2B or C2F (cross 2 back or cross 2 front) = Knit into back (or front) of 2nd st on LHN, then knit first st and slip both sts off LHN.

M1k or M1p (make one knit or make one purl) = Pick up horizontal strand between st just worked and next st on LHN and knit (or purl) into it, as shown in *Basics, Threads No. 43,* p. 26.

T2B (purl back cross) = Sl next st to cable needle (cn) and hold at back of work, k next st, p st from cn.

T2F (purl front cross) = Sl next st to cn and hold at front of work, p next st, k st from cn.

MCB (make cast-on bobble) = Cast on 3 sts into next st on LHN (see *Basics*), and purl these 4 sts. Pass 2nd, then 3rd, then 4th st over first st on RHN—small bobble completed.

---

move? Some patterns call for discreet cables that only cross adjacent groups of right-side knit stitches without involving the background stitches, as shown in my swatches on the facing page, i.e., three knits cross three knits, and the purl stitches between the cables don't move. Since the purl or background stitches are not crossed, they do not need any tension adjustment. In other cable patterns, right-side knit stitches move over right-side purl stitches, so these purl stitches are crossed and require tension adjustments.

Other stitch patterns—To use a pattern with completely incompatible tension, such as a slip stitch, precede it with two rows of garter. Then in the next row, increase or decrease the necessary stitches; the garter hides the adjustment. End the pattern with the complementary adjustment and then two more rows of garter.

Yarn, color, and pattern choices

A light color shows texture best and also makes the work easy to see. Texture doesn't show up as well on a dark color, but neither do mistakes. Texture also shows better on a shiny, smooth yarn than on a matte or textured yarn—on mercerized cotton versus soft wool or mohair—because shiny or smooth raised surfaces catch light best.

After choosing color and yarn, make a tension swatch in stockinette stitch on the needles you plan to use. This will give you accurate enough information for your complex pattern. Don't worry about rows per inch; you'll determine important lengths by measurement.

Knit-in leaves: Space leaves, which require 4 sts, evenly on background of rev st st. Do not count sts on rows 7-16.
Row 1 (RS): p3, k1.
Row 2: p1, k3.
Row 3: p2, C2F.
Row 4: p2, k2.
Row 5: k1, C2F, k1.
Row 6: p4.
Row 7: k1, M1k, k1, M1k, k2.
Row 8: p6.
Row 9: k2, M1k, k1, M1k, k3.
Row 10: p8.
Row 11: k8.
Row 12: p8.
Row 13: sl 1-k1-psso, k3, k2tog, k1.
Row 14: p6.
Row 15: sl 1-k1-psso, k1, k2tog, M1p, k1.
Row 16: p1, k1, p3.
Row 17: sl 1-k2tog-psso, M1p, p1, k1.
Row 18: p1, k3.

Leaves and flowers: Mult. 16 sts, plus 2 sts. Do not count sts on rows 7-16.
Row 1 (RS): *p7, k1,* p2.
Row 2: k2, *p1, k7.*
Row 3: *p6, C2F,* p2.
Row 4: k2, *p2, k6.*
Row 5: *p5, T2B, k1, p4, k1, C2F, k1,* p2.
Row 6: k2, *p4, k4, p1, k1, p1, k5.*
Row 7: *p4, T2B, p1, k2, p3, k1, M1k, k1, M1k, k2,* p2.
Row 8: k2, *p6, k3, p2, k2, p1, k4.*
Row 9: *p4, k1, p2, k1, T2F, p2, k2, M1k, k1, M1k, k3,* p2.
Row 10: k2, *p8, k2, p1, k1, p1, k2, p1, k4.*
Row 11: *p4, k1, p2, k1, p1, k1, p2, k8,* p2.
Row 12: as row 10.
Row 13: *p4, k1, p2, k1, p1, k1, p2, sl 1-k1-psso, k3, k2tog, k1,* p2.
Row 14: k2, * p6, k2, p1, k1, p1, k2, p1, k4.*
Row 15: *p3, MCB, k1, MCB, p1, k1, p1, k1, p2, sl 1-k1-psso, k1, k2tog, M1p, k1,* p2.
Row 16: k2, * p1, k1, p3, k2, p1, k1, p1, k1, sl 1 pwise wyif (with yarn in front), p1, sl 1 pwise wyif, k3.*
Row 17: *p2, MCB, (p1, MCB) 2x, (k1, MCB) 2x, p1, sl 1-k2tog-psso, M1p, p1, k1,* p2.
Row 18: k2, *p1, k4, (sl 1 pwise wyif, p1) 2x, (sl 1 pwise wyif, k1) 2x, sl 1 pwise wyif, k2.*
Row 19: *p2, (p1, MCB) 5x, p3, k1,* p2.
Row 20: k2, *p1, k3, (sl 1 pwise wyif, k1) 5x, k2.*
Row 21: *p7, k1, MCB, p1, MCB, p4, k1, * p2.
Row 22: k2, *p1, k4, sl 1 pwise wyif, k1, sl 1 pwise wyif, p1, k7.*

Different stitch patterns produce different tensions, as the five simple patterns--garter, stockinette, 3 x 3 cable, reverse stockinette, and 1 x 1 rib--on these identical swatches show. You also need to take shade, luster, and texture of a yarn into consideration. A soft, dark wool produces a puffier, less distinct texture than a shiny, light cotton.

shown on the facing page. The single most important factor to remember is that the eye is attracted to the most textured areas. Therefore, place cables, bobbles, and lace very carefully; what fills in around them is less important.

Strive for an overall look of balance and harmony. A harmonic design allows patterns to be repeated, and you should use most of them at least twice on a large garment piece. Cables, bobbles, and lace should be placed with an eye to balance. A large horizontal bobble pattern on the upper right shoulder, for example, can be balanced by smaller vertical ones toward the middle and lower left. But don't misinterpret balance as symmetry, which I try to avoid in this kind of design. And never place the most textured patterns dead center.

Beyond these aesthetic considerations, there are also several practical ones:
• Don't place cables or bobbles where you don't want attention (under the arms, around the hips). Generally, it's wise to keep highly textured patterns between the shoulders and above the waist.
• To avoid dealing with complex patterns and garment shaping at the same time, use simple stitch patterns on sleeve caps, necklines, and armholes.
• Lace should not be used where you do not want to see what is underneath. For example, don't put it on the shoulders if you'll be wearing shoulder pads.

Drawing in the stitch patterns
Begin by drawing your schematic on square-grid graph paper in pencil and on a fairly large scale (half scale or bigger). Note the number of stitches at each width and number of inches at each length, as shown on the facing page.

Keeping design considerations in mind,

draw in your cable stitch patterns (panel **F** in drawing) first because they are the most complex and may need the greatest length for the stitch pattern to be fully developed. Draw them as rectangles that are more or less to scale. If you finish the cable before you reach the allowed length, just fill in with a simple pattern or two. Note the number of stitches that will be allowed from the knitting for each cable stitch pattern and then note, in parentheses, the number of stitches that will have to be added for the tension adjustment.

Then draw in rectangles, and note the number of stitches for your next-most-complex patterns, bobbles and laces (C-E). Try to place them so you do not find yourself working too many unfamiliar or difficult patterns at a time. That would tie you too closely to your instructions, which isn't much fun.

By the time you have finished drawing in the complex patterns, more than half the area of the schematic will be filled. Figure the number of stitches in each of the remaining spaces, and fill them with relatively simple patterns (A-B). Patterns with no fixed repeat, such as moss, garter, and diagonal garter rib can fit almost anywhere. Don't worry about repeating these too often; the simple stitches fade into the background. But do change them often so each covers less area than the complex patterns. Another method of filling spaces that's also a good design strategy is to outline most of the complex patterns. Vertically, I use a single knit stitch; horizontally, I like to use a two-row garter ridge.

The actual knitting
The work should be fun. But knitting so many patterns at the same time will be challenging. Here are some suggestions for making it easier: ⇨

Based on your sts/in. tension, either draft your own pattern schematic or choose a garment pattern that recommends the same tension. In either case, because many other things are going on in this garment, choose a style with minimal shaping.

Layout considerations
After you have a considerable list of compatible stitch patterns and a garment schematic, you can begin the actual design work of putting the two together, as

Making a basic bobble: *For a stockinette bobble on a reverse stockinette ground, work to the bobble stitch. Then increase that one stitch to four by knitting it in front, back, front, and back (above).*

Work three rows of stockinette over these four stitches, ending with a wrong-side row (above).

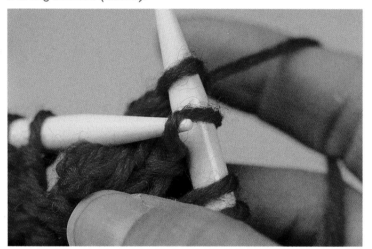

Decrease the four stitches back to one by knitting two stitches together twice (k2tog), then passing the first k2tog over the second (above). Slip the bobble stitch purlwise when you come to it on the next wrong-side row, so it will sit smoothly in the fabric.

A simple approach to mixing textured patterns is to sew separately knit strips of complex patterns together. The strips are easy to knit one at a time, and you don't have to worry about gauge irregularities. (Photo by Yvonne Taylor)

- Familiarize yourself with your stitch patterns before you begin so you won't be too tied to the instructions.
- Photocopy stitch pattern instructions and abbreviations pages before you begin so you won't have to carry heavy books or be caught without the decoding information for something like "T4FL."
- Use stitch markers around patterns you do not readily recognize.
- If a pattern becomes tedious, stop it and do something else. This will improve the design by adding complexity.

- Don't worry too much about mistakes; amidst such chaos, they won't show.
- Remember the "extra" cable stitches when counting stitches.
- If you keep thinking about how difficult this work would be to rip out, you're more likely to remember to get rid of the extra cable stitches after you've completed the final cross.
- Take good care of your drawings and notations; you might want to do this again, and the same drawing can be used for many tensions and sizes. To enlarge, just

draw in a vertical panel of moss here and a horizontal panel of garter there; to reduce, leave some things out.

My original drawn-on-the-bus sketch has seen me through seven of these sweaters. Because the work changes so often, I never tire of this pattern. ☐

Sally Melville of Kitchener, Ont., Canada, teaches writing skills at the University of Waterloo. She also travels to teach advanced knitting and design and many other knitting courses.

Getting the Upper Hand on Intarsia

Three basic techniques will make you a master of multicolor knitting

by Nancy Marchant

intarsia knitting appeals to almost everyone because any image is possible in it, from the geometric ones that I like to use to elaborate pictorial designs, and you can knit with all the beautiful colors you want. But if you've only done a little intarsia and have not yet mastered the technique, you may already have given up on it. It takes patience and practice to learn how to handle many balls, bobbins, or butterflies of different colors of yarn in a single row. And preventing holes from forming between color changes is also a learned skill.

Every color in this sweater is knit with its own tiny ball of yarn. When you've learned how to weave in the ends as you go and how to change colors securely, knitting intarsia can be a lot of fun. The pattern for Nancy Marchant's "Five Triangles Stacked" pullover begins on p. 71. (Winter Night colorway shown in detail above.) (Photo by Susan Kahn) ·

I've spent years refining my intarsia techniques and learning to make them as easy as possible for myself and the knitters who work up my designs. I'd like to share some of my methods for twisting to prevent holes, handling the many lengths of yarn involved, and starting and ending colors.

Twisting yarns

Different books describe the technique of twisting the yarns at each color change to prevent holes differently, but if you study the pictures, they all boil down to the same thing: Intarsia knitting is really ideal for people who prefer to carry the yarn in their right hand. This is because when you finish knitting (or purling) with a color, you just drop it and reach under it with your right hand to take up the next color. This simple action puts a half twist between the yarns when you knit the next stitch because it brings the new color around, to the right, and over the old color, as shown in the left-hand drawings below. If the new yarn is already on the right-hand side of the old color (because you knit past it), just pick it up and knit with it; there won't be a hole. Knitters who hold the yarn in their left hand will need to pick up the new color with their right hand and transfer it to the left hand.

Preparing the colors

Every separate occurrence of every color in intarsia knitting requires its own little ball. Here's how to determine the approximate lengths you'll need for each design element in your pattern (i.e., in this sweater one-, two-, three-, four-, and five-triangle blocks and ribbing triangles) as you knit your patterned gauge swatch: For each color or pattern element in the 6-in. or larger swatch, tie a knot every yard. Then as you knit, count the number of knots you pass and multiply them by 36 in.; subtract the length that remains to the next knot from 36, and add it to the previous number.

But don't cut all the lengths before you need them: If you're knitting with different kinds of yarn, thicker ones will require somewhat more length and thinner ones somewhat less than your average gauge swatch indicated. I always add a selvage stitch at each edge on every piece so that the design won't be affected by seaming; these extra stitches will also require extra length. Besides, you might want to change your pattern or color while you're knitting.

I usually wind my premeasured yarn lengths into butterflies, as shown in the right-hand drawings below, to keep them from tangling. These small, center-pull skeins make handling the many lengths of yarn in an intarsia sweater much easier than just letting the yarn ends dangle, unless the lengths are very short.

Weaving in ends

One knitter who works for me likes to weave in all her ends around the carried-up threads with a crochet hook or tapestry needle when the knitting is finished, as shown in drawing 3 on the facing page, but most knitters find finishing easier if they've already knit in all the starting ends of each color. To ensure invisibility of woven-in ends, I try to weave them in only on top of their own color, which means that not all starting ends can be knit in into the first row, and all finishing ends must be woven in by hand later. I keep a crochet hook that is one size smaller than the knitting needles I'm using in my basket so that whenever I feel like it, I can stop knitting and relax a bit by weaving in ends. If there's intarsia in the ribbing, you need to weave in those ends a little more securely so you can cut the tails short.

Drawings 1, 2, 4, and 5 on the facing page show four ways to begin and knit in ends. There are several variables you need to deal with: Will you have several stitches of the new color behind which the end can be woven on its first row (drawing 1)? Or will you have only one stitch? In that case, you must weave the tail up the side of the new color area as you twist yarns for the color change (drawing 2). Weave the tail along the side at which it exits the first stitch. Is the yarn hairy or textured so that it will stay where it is put? Or is it slippery so that weaving it in requires a bit more care (drawing 4)? And finally, is the yarn thinner or thicker than its fellows? If it's thin, you can use the doubled stitch method shown in drawing 5, which is the easiest weaving-in technique but often adds too much bulk. ☐

Nancy Marchant's article on designing sweaters with repeating motifs appears on pages 74-79. The pattern that follows is the result of the great demand that article originally incited.

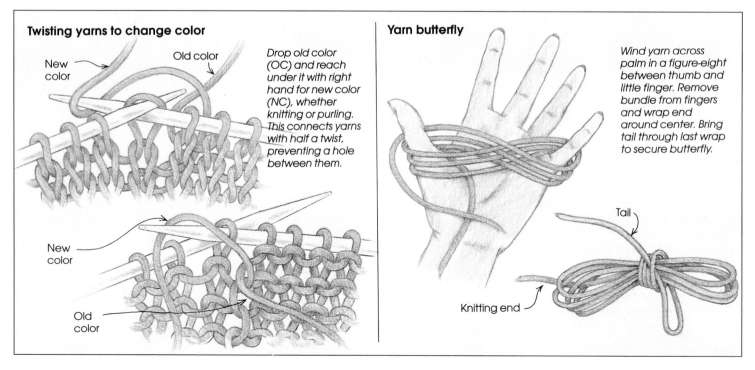

Twisting yarns to change color

New color

Old color

New color

Old color

Drop old color (OC) and reach under it with right hand for new color (NC), whether knitting or purling. This connects yarns with half a twist, preventing a hole between them.

Yarn butterfly

Wind yarn across palm in a figure-eight between thumb and little finger. Remove bundle from fingers and wrap end around center. Bring tail through last wrap to secure butterfly.

Tail

Knitting end

Working in ends

1. Beginning a new color of several stitches

To knit first st, lay NC yarn around RHN with tail hanging to back between needles. Knit first st of NC leaving 2-in. tail. Insert RHN to knit next st, bring tail under, then over OC and NC, then wrap NC and knit (this crosses tail once and prevents hole between colors). Bring NC under tail to cross it when knitting third st, then over tail for fourth. Tail is now woven in. Leave at least ½ in. hanging in back so it won't peek through.

Ball
Tail
OC

2. Beginning a new color with one stitch

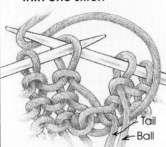

Tail
Ball

Weave tail in over several rows, crossing tail in when you twist threads in a color change and carrying tail up knitting. Weave tail in toward direction it came from to keep first st from twisting when you knit st above it.

3. Weaving in ends with a crochet hook

To prevent hole, hook thread first into carried thread of color next to or above its own color. Then hook thread through and around carried threads of its own color along color-change line. (Photo above)

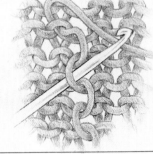

4. Beginning a slippery yarn

Tail
Ball
OC

Tie fat knot in end. Knit first st. Cross tail under OC, then pick up both tail and NC together, and knit next st with both ends. Cross tail with NC for next 2 to 3 sts as above. On next row, treat double-thread stitch as a single-thread st. After weaving in final end, tie fat knot in it too.

5. Beginning a thin yarn

Knit first st of NC as usual. Work next 2-3 sts with both ends of NC. On next row, treat double-thread sts as if they were single-thread sts.

Nancy Marchant's Five Triangles Stacked Pullover

This unisex, medium-weight, geometric-patterned intarsia pullover is shown in two colorways—autumn afternoon and winter night. Each uses 13 different colors. Colored triangles on all the ribbings add a sophisticated touch, but the geometric nature of the intarsia pattern makes it suitable for intermediate knitters with modest intarsia experience.

YARN REQUIREMENTS

The pullover is knit with Scottish Heather, 100% Shetland wool (2-oz. ball = 120 yd.), from Tomato Factory Yarn Co. (8 Church St., Lambertville, NJ 08530), which carries kits for both colorways. You'll need three balls of main color (MC on chart at lower right, p. 72), two balls of A, and one ball each of B through L. Any worsted-weight yarn with a suitable range of colors can be substituted. Choose one with similar yardage, and swatch carefully to obtain the same gauge.

Needles: One pair each, sizes 4, 6, and 8, or size to obtain gauge. One crochet hook, size G or 6. A blunt tapestry needle.

Gauge: To save time take time to check gauge. On size 8 needles, 16 sts and 21 rows equal 4 in. in pattern.

MEASUREMENTS

Directions are given for two sizes—medium and (large). The fit can range anywhere from fairly close fitting to oversized, depending on your preference. See the chart and schematic drawing on p. 72.

Step-by-step instructions

NOTES

Except for ribbings, the entire sweater is knit in stockinette stitch, and the main color thread is carried behind the colored triangles only in the neckband.

Use lengths of yarn for all color areas, but cut the lengths only as you need them. At the beginning of the body pattern, you stack one, two, three, four, or five triangles on top of each other (see the numbers on the bottom triangles on the chart on p. 73). From then on, you always have five triangles stacked, except at the end. If the chart indicates a new color for stitches that will be bound off immediately (i.e., the second group of bind-off sts on the right shoulder, med size), don't change color.

Recommended yarn lengths: Ribbing: Every colored triangle = 22 in.; every main color triangle = 17 in. *Body:* Every 1 triangle = 26 in.; 2 triangles = 50 in.;

3 triangles = 75 in.; 4 triangles = 100 in.; 5 triangles = 125 in. For selvage color areas, add 4 in. per triangle.

Wind cut lengths into butterflies (as shown at lower right on p. 70) to prevent their tangling.

BACK

With size 4 needles and color A, cast on 80 (92) sts.

Begin ribbing: row 1 on chart (WS), and work to row 14 (last row of ribbing). On next row (WS), inc 6 (8) sts evenly across, purling all sts—86 (100) sts.

Body: Change to size 8 needles and follow chart until a total of 133 (145) rows have been worked, or desired length to shoulder; end WS.

Shoulder shaping: Bind off 10 (12) sts at beg of next 4 rows; then bind off 9 (11) sts at beg of next 2 rows. Bind off rem 28 (30) sts.

FRONT

Work same as back until 123 (133) rows have been worked, or desired length to center front neck; end WS.

Neck shaping: Knit 36 (42) sts in pat; bind off 14 (16) sts—red line on chart; cont in pat to end of row.

Right front neck: Next row (WS): Pat to neck edge. *At neck edge—RS rows:* bind off 3 sts once; bind off 2 sts once; bind off 1 st at beg of RS row twice—29 (35) sts. Work 2 (4) rows even; end at side edge (RS row).

Right front shoulder: Bind off 10 (12) sts at beg next 2 WS rows; then bind off 9 (11) sts at beg next WS row. Work RS rows even.

Left front neck and shoulder: Return to sts left on needle. With WS facing, rejoin yarns at neck edge. Bind off 3 sts, and pat to end. Complete to match right side, reversing all shaping.

SLEEVES

With size 4 needles and color A, cast on 50 (56) sts. Follow blue line (green line) on chart, beginning with row 1 for ribbing. At row 15 (WS), purl all sts, increasing 4 (6) sts evenly across—54 (62) sts.

Change to size 8 needles and cont in pat, inc 1 st each side every 8 rows, 10 (11) times—74 (84) sts. Cont until 105 (117) total rows, or desired length. Bind off loosely.

Repeat for second sleeve.

FINISHING

Weave in ends. Lightly steam on WS to relax the work; do not steam ribbings.

Sew front and back together at left shoulder (see *Basics, Threads* No. 42, p. 18, for mattress stitch).

Neckband: With RS facing, size 6 needles, and color A, pick up along back neck 28 (30) sts to left shoulder seam, 25 (26) sts from shoulder seam to center front, 25 (26) sts from center front to end—78 (82) sts. Follow top chart, facing page, using color lengths of 12 in. (row 1 is WS). On row 2 and following rows, carry main color (MC) across back of work. Row 12: Bind off loosely and weave in ends.

Seams: Sew front to back at right shoulder, including neckband. Fold neckband to inside and stitch down loosely.

Sew on sleeves matching center line of sleeve with shoulder seam. Sew sides and underarms in continuous seams matching pattern.

Sweater schematic

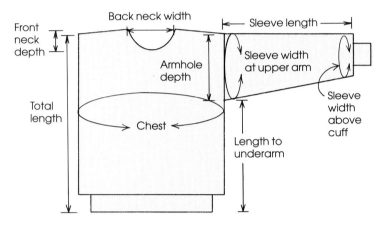

Pullover measurements (in inches)	Medium	Large
Chest	43	50
Total length from lower edge to shoulder	25	27½
Armhole depth	9¼	10½
Length to underarm	15¾	17
Sleeve length	19	21
Sleeve width above cuff	13½	15½
Sleeve width at upper arm	18½	21
Back neck width	7	7½
Front neck depth	3	3½

Key to colorways		
	Autumn Afternoon	**Winter Night**
MC	Moss 1019	North Sea 758
A	Midnight 1163	Hydrangea 1174
B	Anthracite 743	Wilkinson 1315
C	Quartz 1390	Cornflower 1258
D	Mallard 1432	Night Hawk 1471
E	Water Cricket 1042	Iris 857
F	Burnt Umber 890	Highland Mist 1011
G	Ginger 971	Amethyst 690
H	Loganberry 066	Midnight 1163
I	Autumn 998	Mallard 1432
J	Wood Nymph 1517	Duck Egg 1443
K	Peat 744	Aster 1091
L	Brass 1009	Purple Haze 1335

CHART FOR "FIVE TRIANGLES STACKED" BODY, SLEEVES, AND NECKBAND

Neckband chart   *Charts shown as seen from RS.*

Knit
Purl

Row 1 (WS)

Row 12

Lg   Med   Lg   Med   Lg   Med

Center front   Left shoulder

MC

A (Pick-up sts)

Body and sleeve chart

For large size, delete selvage sts of med size (shown in red).

Neck and shoulder shaping for both sizes shown in red.

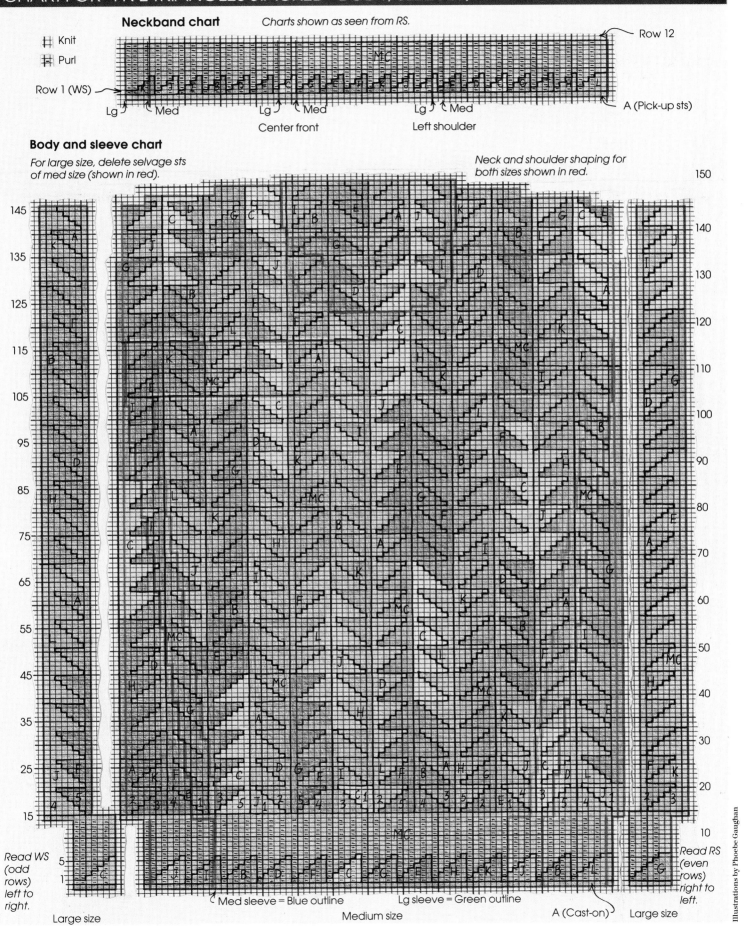

Read WS (odd rows) left to right.

Large size

Med sleeve = Blue outline

Lg sleeve = Green outline

Medium size

A (Cast-on)

Read RS (even rows) right to left.

Large size

Illustrations by Phoebe Gaughan

Smarter than the Average Sweater

Invent refreshing designs with repeating motifs in every color and yarn

by Nancy Marchant

think about sweater designing as a progressive art, and you'll find infinite variation in some very basic ideas. One-color pullovers in stockinette stitch are the simplest to design, but you can make them more interesting by using purl stitches, cables, bobbles, anything. By adding another color to further vary and compound a primary design concept, you can begin to see the enormous potential of every additional color and stitch change. Suddenly, your once basic pullover design has expanded into new and exciting possibilities for you to explore.

I was taught by my parents (I'm from the Midwest) never to throw anything away—not even 30 inches of leftover yarn–"You never know when you'll need that particular piece." Since I've been knitting seriously for more than 20 years, I have accumulated quite a collection of "leftovers." I also have an insatiable appetite for buying yarns. If I "happen" across a yarn store, I want every color of each type of yarn in the place; I have found, however, that I can satisfy this appetite somewhat by buying one ball each of several different yarns. I have also scoured second-hand stores for partial balls of yarn or unfinished sweaters. Once, I found 10 balls of 100% angora in a Goodwill store for 50 cents! As you can well imagine, my studio looks like a yarn shop—chock-full of one ball each of almost every type and color of yarn imaginable. Some balls of yarn date back 40 years!

Until recently, all my magazine knitwear designs had to adhere to strict standards of knitability: They had to be in fashion and fun and quick to knit, and they had to provide step-by-step instructions and use readily available yarns so that knitters could du-plicate the model sweater exactly. Fortunately, glorious knitters like Kaffe Fassett have introduced the "creative-designer" idea to handknitting, and knitters are now becoming more interested in working with original ideas, rather than following exact patterns. This trend in knitwear design has at last freed me of my guilt for not using my wonderful yarn collection. Thus I began to design "leftover" sweaters for *Ariadne*, a Dutch knitting magazine.

I particularly enjoy designing "leftover" sweaters made up of a repeated motif but using many colors. Such an approach allows you to use all your leftover and single balls of yarn. This is how my design process works: First, I develop a repeating motif and chart it on graph paper. Then I select colors and yarns, knit a gauge swatch, and finally draw up a good working pattern of the garment in color.

Developing a repeating motif

Usually, I choose geometric shapes for my repeating motif, such as triangles, rectangles, or squares. There are, of course, numerous ways to give a shape another dimension. For example, let's take a square, as shown on p. 76. Make a line drawing of very large squares or very small squares. Separate the squares, and you create a background. Surround large squares with small squares, draw lines through the squares, overlap the squares, shift them into a brick-laying pattern, turn them 45 degrees to create a diamond shape, put squares inside of squares, elongate them, squash them, cut off their corners to make octagons. Try combining several alternatives.

Make sketches of simple sweater fronts and sleeves using these repeated motifs. It is important to duplicate the scale of the motif to the garment in your sketches. Perhaps you will want to use one motif for the body of the sweater and another for the sleeves. I like to use different motifs on the back and front of vests, as shown at right and in the center photo on p. 77. After selecting your repeated motif, draw it on graph paper, again duplicating the scale to be used in the garment. Don't forget that the "lines" separating each shape in your repeated motif can also be charted, as I've done in my "Jigsaw Puzzle" pullover shown at right and in the bottom photo, p. 77.

I use a graph paper with a 2 to 3 ratio, 8 spaces per in. across and 12 spaces per in. up and down. This type of graph paper provides a more realistic picture of finished knitted work. See p. 79 for sources for knitters' graph paper.

Selecting colors and yarns

The next step is choosing the colors and yarns. While I'm designing the repeated motifs, a color range usually comes to mind. Try to picture using many different reds in one large square next to another large square filled with many different purples. Imagine small squares in different shades of grey. Try to conceive squares inside of squares using soft pastel colors. Perhaps you like the colors in the fabric of a skirt or a Peruvian textile, or maybe you have a beautiful yarn you want to use.

Lately, I tend to pick just one color with which to work. For example, if I pick red, I go through all my red yarns selecting thick, thin, textured, tweeded, bouclés and worsted wools, mohairs, chenilles, and silks, in shades and tints from light red-pink to medium red and on to dark red-burgundy. Dyeing different types and colors of yarns together in one dye bath is also a good way

From *Threads* magazine (October 1990) 31:56-61

Nancy Marchant's garment shapes are simple, but her stunning designs take full advantage of the play between colors and shapes. (Photo by Yvonne Taylor)

Playing with squares

Draw a large square on graph paper; break into smaller squares.

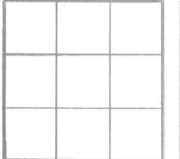 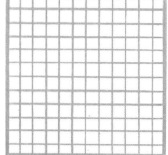

Enclose large squares in smaller squares.

Draw horizontal and vertical lines to break into a plaid.

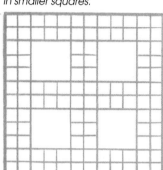 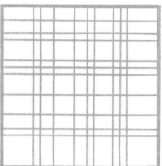

Make squares inside of squares.

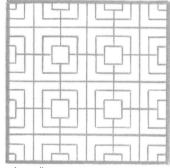

Combine large and small squares.

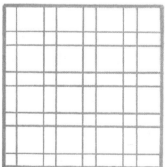 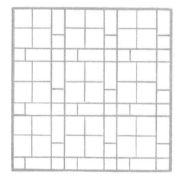

Change squares to rectangles and arrange like bricks.

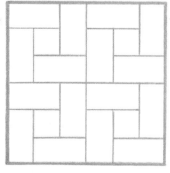

Add spaces between squares to create background.

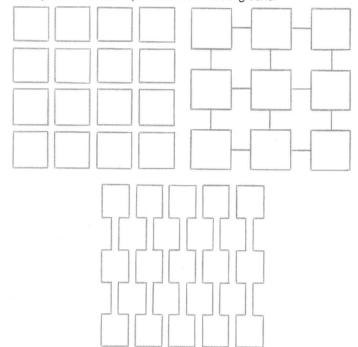

Turn the squares 45° to make diamonds, divide into triangles, or cut off corners for octagons.

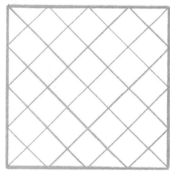 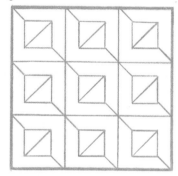

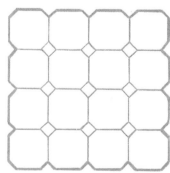

Draw lines to make squares irregular shapes.

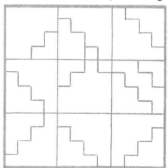 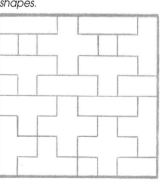

Illustration by Christine Charbonneau

to achieve a one-color range. I try to use a variety of yarns in one garment, but I usually avoid synthetics.

I also like to use a two-color range such as green to blue-green to blue, or blues fading into browns. In this case, I try to incorporate hues of the same intensity. The "Tree" sweater shown at right uses a three-color range from greens, through blues, to violets. When using only one- or two-color ranges, I sometimes add a high-contrast color, such as orange with the green to blue combination, as you can see on the back of my "Fish" vest shown on p. 75.

You might also decide to knit a repeated motif placed on a single background color, as I did on the front of the "Fish" vest. In that case, I like to select the background color first and then the other colors with which to complement or accentuate it.

When selecting your yarns, it's a good idea to choose those with a somewhat similar weight and size. For example, use yarns that can be knit on needle sizes 3 to 5. Of course, you can knit two thin yarns together to obtain the desired size. Combining yarns is also a good way to brighten or dull a color. For instance, if you need to push a pink toward red, simply knit a thin red yarn—it could even be a sewing thread—together with your pink yarn. When purchasing yarns for a "leftover" sweater, try several colors of one type or brand together with several of another type. There is no need to worry about matching dye lots, unless you want an even background color.

I group the balls of yarns together on the floor or in a large basket, pull out colors that clash, and add other yarns to balance my color and yarn combination. I generally use 15 to 20 different yarns and a repeated motif scaled to allow each yarn to be used four or five times on each knitted piece.

Knitting a gauge swatch

Using the yarns I've selected and the charted repeat motif, I make a tension gauge swatch. If the yarns range from needle sizes 3 to 5, I use size 4 needles for the sample and garment. If you are going to use textured stitches in your garment, include them in your gauge swatch to ensure a correct measurement.

"Leftover" knitting requires using the intarsia knitting method in which yarn is worked back and forth, each in its color area. It's important to twist the two yarns together at each color change to avoid gaps, as shown in the drawing at left on p. 78.

In addition to giving you an accurate gauge, sample-making will also tell you whether you need to work with small lengths of yarn (up to 3 yards), wind medium lengths into "fishes" (up to 10 yards), or use whole balls of yarn to fill your color

Two of Marchant's favorite designs involve interlocking shapes: Triangles for the "Tree" sweater and squares for the "Jigsaw Puzzle" pullover. Both are edged in "bobble rib." (Photo by Yvonne Taylor)

On the front of her "Plaid" vest, shown wrong side out, Nancy Marchant uses intarsia with horizontal and vertical lines to divide large squares into smaller ones. The back of the vest is worked in Fair Isle patterns. When she redrew her squares into interlocking puzzle pieces (below), Marchant assigned a stitch to each dividing line. Working them all in the same neutral gray adds harmony.

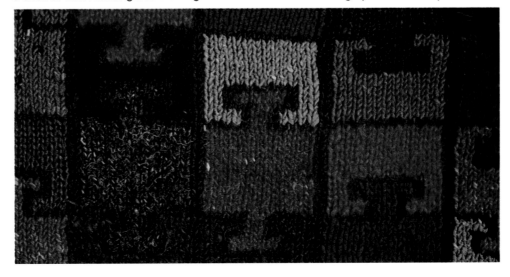

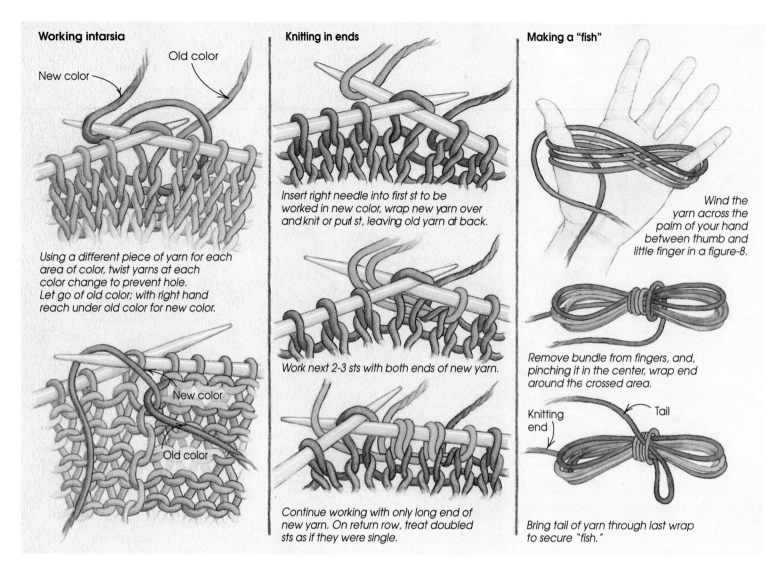

Working intarsia

New color

Old color

Using a different piece of yarn for each area of color, twist yarns at each color change to prevent hole. Let go of old color; with right hand reach under old color for new color.

New color

Old color

Knitting in ends

Insert right needle into first st to be worked in new color, wrap new yarn over and knit or purl st, leaving old yarn at back.

Work next 2-3 sts with both ends of new yarn.

Continue working with only long end of new yarn. On return row, treat doubled sts as if they were single.

Making a "fish"

Wind the yarn across the palm of your hand between thumb and little finger in a figure-8.

Remove bundle from fingers, and, pinching it in the center, wrap end around the crossed area.

Knitting end

Tail

Bring tail of yarn through last wrap to secure "fish."

areas. When making your swatch, mark one-yard lengths on each piece of yarn with a knot, and simply subtract what is left from 36 in. when the sample is finished to determine how many inches of each color you need in one repeat. Larger repeats may require more than one yard, so keep track of the number of knots (yards) and portions you have used. Remember that thicker yarns require a little more length. You can also rip out your gauge swatch, after carefully measuring and noting your stitches and rows, to find the necessary lengths. If your repeated motif is large and you would like to use several yarns in one color area, simply cut easy-to-handle lengths as you knit.

Charting the pattern

After measuring your gauge swatch, calculate the garment pattern, attempting to end with a whole or half motif at the seams. Do this by centering either the middle of one motif or locating the piece's center between two motifs. You may need to add or subtract a few stitches to the garment pattern or adjust your motif by a stitch or two.

I always add one extra stitch to each side edge for selvage.

I feel that the beauty of these sweaters lies in the knit design, not in the garment design, so I usually stick to simple, straight-cut models and avoid complicated collars or shaping.

I chart the entire sweater on my special graph paper in order to see the total result, and then I color it in as much as possible. It is, of course, too difficult to try to color in 20 different reds. When this is the case, I fill my areas with a light, a medium, or a dark red marker and choose the light, medium, or dark red yarns as I am knitting. My front and back pieces almost never match exactly.

When I am using a high-contrast color, I fill in that color first to assure an even balance. If you have half motifs at your side edges, remember to use the same yarn for each corresponding half motif so that the yarns match when the seams are sewn up.

When my charted pattern is complete, I begin my knitting with an interesting rib involving several of the yarns, as shown in the detail photos on the facing page. Some-

times I use a bobble rib (top photo). This is simply a modified seed stitch checkerboard. I alternate two stitches knit in one color with two knit in another. Every second row I purl the contrasting colored stitches, and on the next row the color blocks change position. I also like the elegance of a patterned hem worked in stockinette, as shown in the next two photos. The vertical stripe of Fair Isle corrugated rib produces a strong effect. Alternate two knit stitches in one color with two purl stitches in another, and change the color of the knit stitches symmetrically along the height of the rib, as shown in the fourth picture. If you want your rib to be elastic, thus giving more shape to the sweater, use a k2, p2 rib in wool—creating horizontal stripes by changing yarns every two rows, as shown at bottom.

As you begin knitting the body of the sweater, cut the appropriate lengths or prepare "fishes" (see the drawing above) of each yarn that you will need for the first row. Don't cut your lengths ahead of time because you might want to change a color or your pattern later. I've found that I can simplify cutting when my repeated motif uses yarns of the same length, such as 20 in., as in the "Tree" sweater or the "Fish" vest, by measuring 20 in. and marking it on the arm of my knitting chair with color-headed pins. Thus I can easily measure the cut lengths as I go. Weave in your ends as much as possible while you are knitting, as shown in the center drawing, facing page. Untangling the yarns is easy; the lengths are usually short enough that you can just pull them out.

Study your work as you progress, and make sure that you can see all the yarns you've selected while you're knitting—especially if you are choosing colors as you go along. I use large flat baskets or several transparent plastic bags and separate my yarns by color.

When finishing your garment, match motifs as you are sewing up the seams, and try to make your neckband as interesting as the other ribbing.

Sometimes when I am proudly wearing one of my "leftover" sweaters, I notice a yarn that I used in another sweater for someone dear to me, or I recognize a yarn that I purchased on one of my sprees in a foreign country. Every yarn has a tale to tell. It is at those moments that I appreciate saving my leftovers. □

Nancy Marchant has been a fiber professional specializing in surface design and knitting for the last 15 years. Now living in Amsterdam, her designs appear regularly in Ariadne *and* Vogue Knitting.

Sources for knitters' graph paper

Krüh Knits
Box 1587
Avon, CT 06001
*8½ x 11 in. pad of 30 sheets,
8 sts and 11 rows in., $4.95 + S&H.
Catalog, $3.*

Patternworks
Box 1690
Poughkeepsie, NY 12601
(914) 462-8000
*8½ x 11 in. pad with 10 sheets,
5 sts/in., $2.25 + S&H.*

Schoolhouse Press
6899 Cary Bluff Rd.
Pittsville, WI 54466
(715) 884-2799
*8½ x 11 in. pad with 25 sheets,
5 sts and 7 rows/in. or 8 sts and
11.2 rows/in., $3.50 + S&H.*

Studio or White knitting machine dealers

For the dealer nearest you write:
VWS
11760 Berea Rd.
Cleveland, OH 44111
*Large 25-sheet pad with 200 sts x 200
rows, 11 sts and 14 rows/in., retails for $16.95.*

Nancy Marchant likes interesting ribbings. Her bobble rib is a modified seed stitch checkerboard in two or three colors.

Patterned stockinette hems add a fancy touch, with or without fringe.

Fair Isle corrugated k2, p2 rib, in which the colors change on the knit columns, can be very effective

Changing the colors every two rows in a k2, p2 rib produces an elastic, colorful edge.

Working with Alpaca

This lustrous fiber combines the qualities of silk and wool

by Julie Owens

*t*en years ago, when I was commissioned to knit an alpaca sweater, I dreaded it because my memory of alpaca was of the scratchy commercial sweaters from decades before. But the yarn turned out to be soft and silky, and the result of my knitting was luxurious and beautiful. I wondered why the fiber seemed so different, and because I spin, weave, and sew, as well as knit, I began to explore the properties of alpaca yarns and fibers. You'll find my hand- and machine-knitting pattern for the white scarf shown at left on p. 83.

Alpaca, the animal

Alpacas and llamas, members of the *Camilidae* family, do not occur in a wild state; their development started as early as 1500 B.C. when the pre-Incan peoples began taming the wild guanaco. They are still raised primarily in Bolivia and Peru at elevations of 12,000 ft. to 16,000 ft. Virtually all commercially processed fiber and yarn comes from South America, primarily from the suri and the more numerous huacaya alpacas. See "Alpacas in the north" on the facing page for information about North American alpacas.

Fiber characteristics

The fleece of the huacaya is stronger, somewhat crimped, and appears fluffy; it feels slightly harsh compared to a suri fleece. The luster of huacaya fiber is similar to the luster of wool produced by Romney sheep, and it reacts to the chemicals used for commercial processing and dyeing much as wool does. Suri fiber is straight and uncrimped or slightly wavy. It is less lustrous and is very sensitive to chemicals. Yarn spun from huacaya is loftier and lighter in weight than suri yarn of similar diameter because of the crimp. Even so, suppliers of alpaca yarns or top for spinning do not distinguish between the two types. Thus, brown fiber from different sources could be vastly different. The only thing you can be relatively sure of is that dyed fiber or yarn is huacaya.

Alpacas come in a wide variety of colors: from snowy white and pearly blue-grays to inky blacks and from creamy beige, cinnamon, and browns to warm brown-blacks. Their fiber is lightweight, with a high insulation value.

The rich multicolors of a roan alpaca fleece make it ideal for handspinning variegated yarn that weaves as a random plaid. Julie Owens knit her white lace scarf with a commercial alpaca yarn; the pattern is on p. 83. (Photo by Susan Kahn)

From *Threads* magazine (December 1991) 38:46-49

Alpaca fiber for the handspinner—You can buy alpaca as fleece or commercial top (see "Sources" on p. 82). U.S. fleece starts at about $3.50/oz. or $56/lb.

Commercial top, which is ready to spin immediately, averages $40/lb. and has virtually no weight loss. But because of the variation in its fiber characteristics, I prefer using domestic fleece. Alpaca breeders are usually willing to send fleece samples for a small fee, which they may refund with a fleece purchase. If you're buying alpaca fleece, be sure that you and the breeder agree ahead of time that if the fleece is received in an exceptionally dirty or otherwise unacceptable state, you can return it for a full refund.

Another reason I prefer fleece to top is that the fiber is not totally blended. Although a given top may look quite heathered, it won't spin like a roan fleece, which is composed of several colors but at a distance appears gray or light cinnamon. Generally, the lighter the color, the greater the fiber diameter. In a gray roan fleece you'll have very fine black fibers, medium-fine gray fibers, and slightly coarser white fibers. When spun from the lock, the coarser fibers will draft out first: white, gray, then finally black—resulting in a variegated yarn. I use this yarn to weave scarves that look like a random plaid but are nothing more than plain weave, as shown on the facing page.

Alpaca yarns—Commercial yarns do not differ greatly from well-made handspun yarns. The most noticeable difference is uniformity of color. But due to the harsh chemicals used in industrial processing, commercially dyed yarns may be weaker than handspun, hand-dyed yarns.

Dyeing alpaca—White and off-white fibers dye well with a good wool dye such as Telana, available from Earth Guild (33 Haywood St., Asheville, NC 28801; 800-327-8448). Intense colors seem to require a bit more dye than wool, but the color range is just as great. Yarns spun from fleece dye as easily as those from top, and both forms of fiber dye well unspun. Alpaca yarn from Henry's Attic (5 Mercury Ave., Monroe, NY; 914-783-3930, for nearest supplier) dyes as easily as handspun. I have never tried to dye or over-dye knitting yarns because the chemicals used on commercially spun fiber could alter the effectiveness or color of the dye.

Weaving with alpaca yarns—Alpaca does not behave like wool, so it is essential that you weave samples and finish them with the same techniques you intend for the final yardage. Alpaca's lack of shrinkage makes it a lot of fun for designing. When you weave stripes or plaids that alternate alpaca and fine wool, and finish the fabric in the washer and dryer under controlled conditions, you'll produce delightful seersuckers.

Sewing with alpaca yardage—Yardage, whether handwoven or commercially manufactured, needs special considera-tion when you're planning garment structures and construction methods. Because alpaca yarns do not easily felt and are inherently slippery, cut edges tend to fray. So they need immediate protection. On all cut edges, I use either serger overcasting or machine straight stitching with zigzagging outside the straight stitch. Fabric of 100% alpaca fiber is quite slippery, and seams should be basted or heavily pinned before sewing. It is also wise to avoid garments with sharp points and angles such as lapels, welt pockets, and collars.

Woven alpaca can be hand laundered or dry cleaned; follow manufacturers' guidelines. I usually dry-clean tailored items. If you're testing the hand-washability of yardage, be sure to take accurate measurements to determine possible shrinkage, and watch for dye release. Remember that garments of mixed fiber may felt and/or pucker if subjected to extreme temperature changes and agitation during washing and rinsing.

Knitting with alpaca yarns

Because alpaca lacks crimp, alpaca yarns do not bounce back the way wool yarns do. In fact, alpaca yarns hang limply as do many silk, angora, cotton, and linen yarns. To make sure your finished sweater won't stretch, knit and finish generous swatches by hand or machine. Launder, block, dry, and finish the swatches the same way the final garment will be handled. If the item is to be dry cleaned, don't launder the sample; steam

Alpacas are nearly perfect fleece-bearing animals—intelligent, even-tempered, and beautiful. This roan animal is ready for shearing. (Photo by Meadowlark Farm)

Alpacas in the north
by Gretchen Quigg

The alpaca's appeal is obvious: small (about 3 ft. at the shoulder), fuzzy, clean, gentle, intelligent, and curious; it epitomizes "cute."

Until the small importations from Chile in 1983, '84, and '88, alpacas in North America were found only in zoos or as rare exotic pets. Today their population has grown to almost 2,000.

Alpacas were bred to thrive in the demanding environment of the high Andes. They are amazingly hardy and frugal and have adapted easily throughout the altitudes of North America. Because of the relative obscurity of the breed outside South America, little authoritative literature is available. However, as alpaca numbers increase, North American universities are developing alpaca-related research programs.

Alpaca owners in North America are discovering that as delightful as their animals are as pets, they have an intrinsically greater potential. The alpaca breed was developed to produce high-quality fiber for harvest. Breeders have found that their animals must be shorn periodically for health and comfort. And many are beginning to realize that with proper preparation and shearing, they have a commodity of great value to the handspinner. Although (don't press) it to release any distortion. Measure swatches carefully and use exact stitch gauge.

In designing alpaca knits, here are some things to consider: The fiber is very warm, so light, lacy knits are quite toasty. When you make knit garments with sleeves (particularly lacy ones), you need to reinforce the shoulder seams to prevent the weight of the sleeves from stretching them. I either hand stitch narrow satin ribbon across the shoulder seams as a stabilizer, going across the back neck edge as well, if the design permits; or I seam the shoulder firmly with backstitch. I avoid grafted seams at the shoulder in sleeved garments.

Alpaca yarns (commercial or handspun), with their soft, silky, slippery texture, can cause hand and machine knitters a bit of grief because they tend to split easily. Cabled yarns, which are twisted together of two or more two-ply yarns, are less likely to split than plain plied yarns. But the more twist yarns have in both the singles and plied states, the less soft and lofty the finished knitting will be. You'll also have more trouble with splitting if you knit tightly. Try using a smaller needle size and maintaining a looser tension to alleviate the problem. To help cope with splitting, I knit with needles of a color that contrasts with the yarn, use a strong light, and try to knit when distractions are few.

Alpaca yarns work well for machine knitters. I have used several commercial and handspun yarns on a variety of knitting machines with very little difficulty. Of course, if the machine tension is too great, yarn breaks will occur; and if the tension is too little, dropped or split stitches will result. The only problem I have encountered is that commercially dyed yarns tend to break in lace patterns. I don't have this problem with my handspun, hand-dyed alpaca yarn.

I prefer to hand wash my finished alpaca knits, but I dry-clean those that have sewn-in shoulder pads or those of commercially dyed yarn that bleeds color. I place the garment in a sink of warm water to which I've added a little detergent, usually Dawn dishwashing liquid. I soak it for 30 to 60 minutes and then squeeze gently to help remove any soil. I squeeze out excess water and rinse the piece in lukewarm water, repeating until the water remains clear. Then I squeeze out the excess water and roll the garment in terry cloth towels to remove as much moisture as possible. Although they do not tend to felt or shrink, wet alpaca knits are very stretchy and should be supported carefully. Next I lay out the garment to dry flat on a sweater-drying rack or a towel and pat it into shape. After the garment is thoroughly dry, I may decide to give it a light steaming to enhance the pattern stitches. Allow freshly steamed garments to dry thoroughly before handling. □

Julie Owens of Estacada, OR, is a knitter, weaver, and seamstress as well as a spinning instructor.

Sources

Alpaca fleece
Gretchen Quigg and Tom Chamlee
Meadowlark Farm
PO Box 6038
Portland, OR 97228
(503) 283-2524
The breeders I deal with.

Alpaca Owners & Breeders Assn.
c/o Hobert Office Services Ltd.
PO Box 1992
Estes Park, CO 80517
(303) 586-9519
For information about breeders in your area.

Alpaca top and roving
Ready-to-spin alpaca is available from many sources, including local spinning and weaving shops. I have dealt with the following suppliers, some of whom occasionally carry scoured fleece:

The Fiber Studio
9 Foster Hill Rd.
PO Box 637
Henniker, NH 03242
(603) 428-7830

Straw Into Gold
3006 San Pablo Ave.
Berkeley, CA 94702
(415) 548-5243

Woolston's Woolshed
Dept. Th101
651 Main St.
Bolton, MA 01740
(508) 779-5081

---

most alpaca breeders have no wool experience, many are beginning to learn about wool quality and give it some consideration in their breeding programs.

Alpacas produce three to four pounds of wool per year with a staple length of about 4 in. in the main part of the fleece. A two-year growth, staple length of about 8 in., will be in good condition, but wool left on the animal much longer will begin to weather and will become tender and cott (mat) at the tips.

At present, there are no suri alpacas in North America (see p. 80). Most are huacaya, with an estimated 5% chili, an intermediate type with wavier, more hairlike fiber.

See "Sources," above, for information on finding a local alpaca breeder, or contact us. When you have found an owner interested in selling fiber, go out and look at it, preferably while still on the animal. Alpacas love to roll, but since the fleece is fine, dry, and open, debris is more easily removed before shearing by grooming than afterward by picking.

Alpaca fleece is most accurately appraised on the animal. There is a surprising variety of softness, luster, color, crimp, and fiber diameter between animals, and even within the same fleece. As with other wool breeds, an alpaca's first shearing will be its softest, and most young animals are more consistent over their entire fleeces than are adults.

Alpacas have three types of fiber. The softest and most wool-like, often having some crimp (slight by sheep standards) will range from 22 to 29 microns. The locks tend to be "tippy" because of a certain percentage of longer, slightly coarser intermediate fiber. These wavier fibers won't be evident when the yarn is spun. The coarsest fibers are the guard hair, which will inevitably be found in certain areas of the fleece. Rate of growth is roughly proportional to fiber diameter, so the coarser fibers will extend beyond the more wool-like ones.

The best quality wool will be found in the "blanket," which wraps around the animal between the withers (shoulders) and the rump, exclusive of belly wool. The upper part of the neck front tends to be the next best, and the back neck is next in quality, with coarser intermediate fiber. The coarsest fiber is found in the "apron" at the lower front of the neck, legs, and belly. Examine the blanket for guard hair, which, if present, will be most evident at the withers. This will seriously decrease the blanket's value. To check the blanket for consistency, open the fleece at withers, mid-flank, and haunch along the side. Check for similarity of softness, crimp, intermediate fiber, luster, and color.

Gretchen Quigg is co-owner of Meadowlark Farm in Portland, OR.

Alpaca lace scarf

This soft, drapey lace scarf, shown on p. 80, is suitable for the intermediate to advanced knitter. You can make a beautiful version of it if you just knit the leaf pattern as an allover repeat. Julie Owens omitted alternate leaves on the first half-repeat, knit several repeats of the allover pattern, then began omitting leaves selectively, as indicated on the chart below. She knit two identical pieces and grafted them at the center. (*Machine knitters: the "upside-down" key on electronic machines won't produce a mirror image in lace mode.*)

YARN REQUIREMENTS

Three 50g balls of Indiecita sport-weight alpaca (185 yd/ 50g) from Plymouth Yarns. It's widely available in yarn stores, or contact Plymouth Yarn, PO Box 28, Bristol, PA 19007; (215) 788-0459.

Needles: Size 3, or size to get gauge. Size D or 3 crochet hook.
Gauge: 7 sts and 9 rows = 1 in. in stockinette stitch.
Machine tension: 6 on lace; 8 on stockinette. Make the transition over several in. of knitting.
Finished size: 9 in. by 58 in., including fringe.

Step-by-step instructions

HANDKNITTING

Cast on and work over 61 stitches, five repeats of Leaf Pattern or your own variation of it, as suggested by the chart below.

Work one piece 48 in. long and bind off. Or work two identical pieces 24 in. long, the last few in. all stockinette; graft together. Add new balls at the edge.

Notes on lace-making sts: This pattern exploits the slanting properties of decrease stitches and the lacy quality of yarnovers. All stitches are purled on WS rows. There are as many yo's as decs, so stitch count remains constant.
K2tog (knit 2 sts together): is a single decrease slanting right.
Sl1-k1-psso (slip 1-knit 1-pass slipped st over) (see Basics, Threads *No. 38, p. 14*): is a single decrease slanting left.

Sl2tog kwise-k1-p2sso (slip 2 tog knitwise-knit 1-pass 2 slipped sts over) (see Basics, Threads No. 38): is a vertical double decrease with two side sts slanting inward behind prominent center st.
Yo (yarn over): makes a new st with a lacy hole below it.

Leaf Pattern: (Multiple of 12 sts, plus 1 st). Rep rows 1-16.
Row 1 (WS) and all other WS rows: purl.
Rows 2 (RS) & 4: K2tog, *k2, yo, sl 1-k1-psso, yo, k1, yo, k2tog, yo, k2, sl2tog kwise-k1-p2sso; rep from *, end sl 1-k1-psso.
Row 6: K2tog, *k1, yo, k2tog, yo, k3, yo, sl 1-k1-psso, yo, k1, sl2tog kwise-k1-p2sso; rep from *, end sl 1-kl-psso.
Row 8: K2tog, *yo, k2tog, yo, k5, yo, sl 1-k1-psso, yo, sl2tog kwise-k1-p2sso; rep from *, end sl 1-k1-psso.
Rows 10 & 12: K1, *yo, k2tog, yo, k2, sl2tog kwise-k1-p2sso, k2, yo, sl 1-k1-psso, yo, kl; rep from *.
Row 14: K2, *yo, sl 1-k1-psso, yo, k1, sl2tog kwise-k1-p2sso, kl, yo, k2tog, yo, k3; rep from *, end k2.
Row 16: K3, *yo, sl 1-k1-psso, yo, sl2tog kwise- k1-p2sso, yo, k2tog, yo, k5; rep from *, end k3.

MACHINE KNITTING

When using a lace carriage, tension and weights are extremely important, particularly with alpaca. Swatch both lace and stockinette to determine appropriate tension for each.

Cast on and work over 62 stitches. For Knitking and Brother electronic machines, this pattern is preprogrammed, No. 159. Or punch a card or hand manipulate the stitches by referring to the handknitting chart below. For double decs, use 2- or 3-prong transfer tools on both sides of center st. For k2tog before yo or sl 1-k1-psso after yo, work a one-step transfer by moving eyelet st to adjacent dec st. For k2tog after yo or sl 1-k1-psso before yo, work a two-step transfer by moving 2nd st to 1st needle, then both sts to 2nd needle. Yo needles must be in WP; dec needles carry 2 or 3 sts.

FINISHING

Weave in ends. Knot a 5-in.-long fringe on every other cast-on or bind-off st on both ends. Cut two 10½-in.-long strands for each knot. Then work two rows of single crochet along each side to prevent curling. Hand wash and block. –J.O.

Allover leaf lace chart

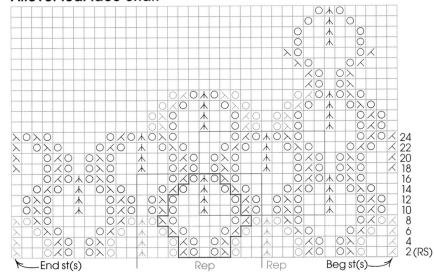

End st(s) Rep Rep Beg st(s)

Work green symbols as stockinette to separate leaves with stockinette areas; work them as charted for allover lace patterning.

Allover lace multiple marked in magenta; repeat rows as many times as desired. Then complete top halves of all isolated or partial leaves (rows 9-16, sts outlined in purple). (Multiple is also marked in green if lace rather than stockinette worked on first eight rows.)

Purple outline marks stitches of single leaf.

Key to symbols for handknitters

☐ K

⊠ K2tog

⊠ Sl 1-k1-psso

⧄ Sl2tog kwise-k1-p2sso

◎ Yo

Row 1 and all odd numbered rows, WS, purl.

Read chart right to left.

Perfect Ribbing for All Fibers

A rib that alternates single and double layers never loses its shape

by June Hemmons Hiatt

ibbing is used on nearly every knitted garment, but the results are sometimes disappointing, particularly if the yarn has poor memory, as do cotton, silk, linen, rayon, alpaca, and many synthetics. The most common problems with ordinary ribs are the ribbing doesn't fit properly, it stretches with wear, and the cast-on edge isn't always as elastic as the fabric. These problems frustrated me for a long time, and I'd like to share the solutions I've developed that make a difference, as you can see on the sweater above.

My new ribbing solution, double-knit rib, begins with a cast-on as elastic as the knitting itself and then alternates a few rows of single rib (k1, p1) with a row or two of double knit. Double knit is a technique that allows you to create two fabric faces at the same time: the even-numbered stitches go to one side and the odd numbered stitches to the other. The resulting fabric is wonderfully resilient with the single rib providing elasticity and the double knit providing stability (and, if desired, channels for elastic). See the examples on p. 86. I also have a few suggestions on gauging how to make your rib fit the body perfectly.

Getting started

You will need five needles: one *very* small one just for casting on (perhaps size 0 or 1) and two pairs in consecutive sizes for the ribbing. You use the smaller pair for the double-knit rows to compensate for the tendency of those stitches to enlarge.

I've also found that any rib looks better if you use a much smaller needle than you normally use. Instead of working the single-rib rows on a needle that's two sizes smaller than the sweater needle, try going down three or four sizes. This will take longer and will use more yarn, but it will give a plush elasticity and a firm texture.

Begin by casting on an even number of stitches in alternating cast-on, as shown on the facing page, using your very thin needle.

Making double-knit ribbing

In single rib the yarn travels from knit to purl to knit, but because of the rib's elasticity, all you really see are the knit stitches on both sides. In double knit, this illusion becomes reality. To make a fabric with two stockinette faces, the yarn travels to alternate stitches on the needle, which draws them closer together, stabilizing the stretch of the single rib.

Double knit—The trick for making a rib that really holds its shape lies with double knit, which creates two right sides at once. You work the stitches of just one fabric face at a time: work every other

At last! a ribbing that does its job even in cotton. The ribbing on this all-cotton sweater continues to hug the model's waist, wear after wear. The trick is to combine double knit and single rib to achieve this miraculous effect.

stitch, slipping the intervening stitches with the yarn stranded between the two fabric faces. To do the other fabric face, you work all the stitches that were slipped on the first side and slip those that were worked, as shown in the drawing on p. 86. In effect, by knitting half the stitches on one side and the other half on the other side, you're really knitting in the round—so there's no purling and it takes two sides to complete one row.

Combining double knit and ribbing—Use my alternating cast-on to put an even number of stitches on the tiny needle. With the larger of the two needle pairs, work one row of single rib in the stitch pattern established by the cast-on. Continue work as follows:
1. Using the smaller needle pair, *work one complete row of double knit* (work each fabric face once).
2. Using the larger needle pair, *work two rows of single rib.* Repeat these two steps for the desired length of the ribbing.

Selvages—If you need selvage stitches for sewing up, cast on two extra stitches. Treat the slip knot as a purl stitch (rather than a knit) and work alternating cast-on, "knit," then "purl." Work the single-ribbing rows in the established pattern, but slip the first stitch knitwise and purl the last stitch on every row.

Elasticized ribbing—As an added bonus, the row of double knit in this ribbing creates a tiny casing through which you can thread yarn elastic. This is the perfect solution for yarns like cotton,

Alternating cast-on for knit 1, purl 1 rib

Alternating cast-on is ideal for single rib because it places alternate knit and purl stitches on the needle. The bottom edge is soft because the cast-on is really the first row, so it's every bit as elastic as the fabric. But to keep it firm, make it on a much smaller needle than the size you intend for knitting.

Cast on an even number of stitches. Allow a length of yarn and make a slip knot (the first knit st). Begin the cast-on sequence purl, then knit as shown.

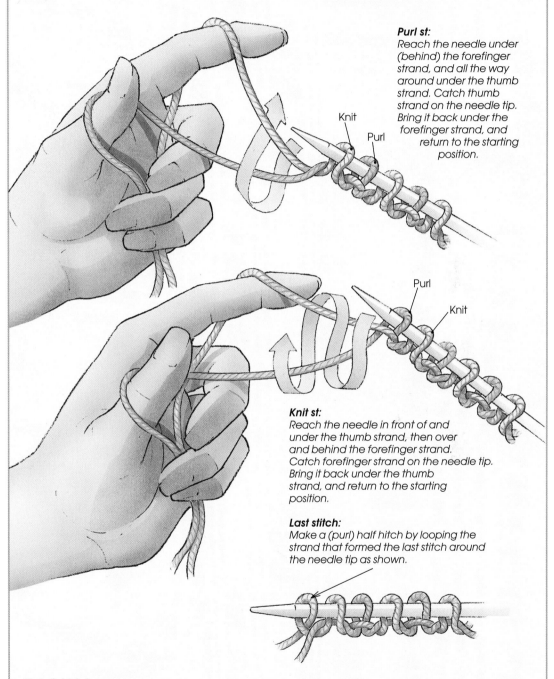

Purl st:
Reach the needle under (behind) the forefinger strand, and all the way around under the thumb strand. Catch thumb strand on the needle tip. Bring it back under the forefinger strand, and return to the starting position.

Knit st:
Reach the needle in front of and under the thumb strand, then over and behind the forefinger strand. Catch forefinger strand on the needle tip. Bring it back under the thumb strand, and return to the starting position.

Last stitch:
Make a (purl) half hitch by looping the strand that formed the last stitch around the needle tip as shown.

Helpful hints

Work very firmly with an even tension. Keep your right forefinger on the last stitch made to hold it in position. Don't let go of the yarns in your left hand, or the last few stitches will begin to unravel. If you need to pause, make a temporary half hitch, but be sure to remove it before you continue.

Notice how the forefinger strand is pulled up on the near side to form a "knit" stitch (with its characteristic V shape) and how the thumb strand is pulled up on the far side for a "purl" stitch.

Until the process becomes second nature, try this helpful chant: "over, under, under, under (purl); over, under, over, under (knit)."

Illustrations by Clarke

Basic double-knit rib looks very even, stretches somewhat less than single-rib, but recovers its shape exactly. For yarns that have poor memory—cotton, silk, and linen—you can run an elastic thread or ⅛-in. elastic through the double knit rows.

Labels on samples: Single rib · Double-knit rib · Double-knit rib, elastic thread · Double-knit rib, ⅛-in. elastic

linen, and silk that stretch easily and often permanently. Wool ribbing is sufficiently resilient without elastic.

You can carry the elastic along as you work, but threading it in later with a tapestry needle helps you control the tension. If you have seams, do this after they have been sewn. The elastic, which is completely hidden when the fabric is relaxed, will show slightly when the ribbing is stretched out, so match the yarn color as closely as possible. (You can order 16 colors of Rainbow Elastic Plus for knitting from Patternworks, PO Box 1690, Poughkeepsie, NY 12601; 914-462-8000.)

If you want to use flat elastic (⅛ to ¼ in. wide), you need to alter the double-knit part of the pattern slightly to make the casing deeper and to leave its selvages open so you can insert the elastic. Cast on and work one row of single rib as described above. Then work the double knit as follows: With the smaller needles work two complete rows (four sides) of double knit, working two rows on one fabric face—first the outside in knit then the inside in purl—then two rows on the other fabric face—first the inside in purl, then the outside in knit—as follows:
Rows 1 & 4: *K 1, bring yarn to near side (yns), sl 1, bring yarn to far side (yfs)*, repeat *-* to end, and turn.
Rows 2 & 3: *Yfs, sl 1, yns, p1*, repeat *-* to end, and turn.
This leaves the left selvage completely open; the right selvage will have a single running thread that you can easily push aside when you

Double knitting

To make a fabric where both sides are stockinette, work every other stitch as follows:

Sides 1 and 2: With an even number of stitches, *knit 1, bring yarn to near side, slip 1 purlwise, return yarn to far side*; repeat *-* to end of row; turn. One double-knit row completed; both sides are stockinette.

Far-side stitches (colored red)
Slip when knitting near side.

Near-side stitches (colored purple)
Slip when knitting far side.

Note: You will knit the single rib knit sts and slip the single rib purl sts.

insert the elastic.

Then work two rows of single rib with the larger needles. Alternate casing and single rib for the desired length of the rib.

Making ribbing that fits

The key to creating perfect ribbing is to make it fit that part of the body it is meant to surround with just the right amount of stretch. This requires a new way of thinking about what ribbing is and what it is supposed to do and a special way of calculating its gauge so you will have the number of stitches that you really need.

Measure the body where the ribbing is supposed to fit (for example: just below the waist, at the high hip, at the low hip, or at the wrist or neck). Now here's how you calculate gauge for a ribbing that hugs gently:

What I call *average gauge for rib* is a gauge that reflects the number of stitches in 1 in. of ribbing when it is stretched out halfway. This puts the fabric under slight tension so it will grip the body, but it is not stretched so tightly that the yarn or the stitch structure is strained.

To make a gauge sample, use alternating cast-on and

work 2 in. of approximately 3-in.-wide ribbing in the double-knit (or plain-rib) pattern you prefer. Break the yarn and thread the stitches onto the tail for a holder. Wash the sample to relax the yarn, and allow it to dry.

When you perform the following calculations, round all numbers to the nearest tenth. *Do not drop tenths.*
1. Place the swatch flat on a table. Use a hard ruler to measure the swatch length from side to side.
2. Divide this measurement into the number of stitches you cast on. Record this *relaxed gauge*.
3. Now, holding one side of the swatch at the ruler end, stretch the swatch as far as possible to remeasure.
4. Divide this measurement into the number of stitches and record the *stretched gauge*.
5. Add the two gauges, then divide by two to get the *average gauge*.

To find the number of stitches that your ribbing requires, multiply the average gauge by the body measurement. Here is where those tenths are important: a difference of only .2 in a 40-in. measurement means eight stitches too many or too few—a 1- to 2-in. difference in circumference, depending on your gauge. □

June Hemmons Hiatt is the author of The Principles of Knitting *(New York: Simon And Schuster, 1988). Chapter 25 of the book includes more information on calculating ribbing, and chapter 13 discusses double knit.*

Putting Stitches in Their Place

Bind on handsome hems and pockets

Attach a separately knit patch pocket so perfectly that the seam is almost invisible. Paula Levy's technique is also excellent for producing very smooth hems and a vast number of decorative attachments and folded effects. (Photo by Susan Kahn)

by Paula Levy

hen all else fails, make something up. Several years ago, I started a top-down sweater with a reverse stockinette rolled neckband. (I started with the band, rolled it outward so the reverse stockinette showed, and knit the cast-on loops together with the body stitches at the base of the band to secure it like a hem.) It never dawned on me that I wouldn't be able to finish the bottom hem to match, but there wasn't a way to do that until I developed the technique I call "putting down stitches" (PDS).

Basically, what I found was that instead of folding the hem to the inside and sewing (the normal method), I could fold the knitting up over the outside, pull the stitches on the needle through to the inside of the sweater, and secure them there. This produced a reverse stockinette roll that exactly matched the one at the neck. I named my technique "putting down stitches" because it's the opposite of "picking up stitches," the technique for creating stitches by pulling loops of yarn through spaces in the fabric from the inside to the outside.

As I've written about and taught PDS, I've come to appreciate just how versatile it is. You don't have to work the hem last in reverse stockinette. You can do the hem first in stockinette and have it join the body with a very subtle line, as shown in the drawings on p. 88. Moreover, the loops don't even have to be stitches; they can also be produced at the bottom and sides of a knit piece. Hems, seams, pockets (above), and assorted other joins can be made invisibly or decoratively with PDS.

Before you begin

PDS isn't difficult to learn, but it does require some rather creative visualization, as shown in the top drawing on p. 88. Instead of folding a hem to the wrong side and attaching it, you fold a PDS hem up over the front. The result is that the wrong side of the bottom section suddenly becomes the right side. So if you want stockinette on the outside, you need to knit the hem allowance in reverse stockinette, then switch back to stockinette for the main fabric.

To do PDS, you use waste yarn that will be removed. Choose one that's thinner than your knitting yarn, plain, and a bit slippery. It should have some color contrast to your project yarn so that you can see it clearly, but not too much, because when you remove the waste yarn, you don't want it to leave colorful little fuzzies in its wake. Use double-pointed or circular needles so you'll never find them pointing in the wrong direction. Swatching is necessary so you can see how various PDS techniques look and feel in your yarn. Besides, experimenting with swatches will help you to be more creative with the technique.

Making a stockinette PDS hem

You make the PDS hem first when you start a sweater from the bottom. Start with an invisible cast-on so that when you're ready to put the hem stitches down, you'll have open loops. I find that provisional crochet cast-on works best (see *Threads* No. 35, p. 20). When you're ready to free the cast-on loops for PDS—

From *Threads* magazine (February 1992) 39:65-67

Making a hem by "putting down stitches"

Parts of a hem

4. Then work k1, p1 rib one row less than hem length to serve as hem backing.

5. Change to regular needles and knit stockinette garment fabric.

3. On smaller needles, work a turning row (lower edge of garment).

2. Work hem in reverse stockinette.

Garment RS

Hem backing RS

Hem WS

Project yarn tail

1. Start with invisible cast-on using provisional crochet method. Leave a tail of project yarn five times as long as project width for finishing.

Preparing to turn hem

Hem RS

1. Undo chain and put cast-on stitches on double-pointed needle.

Garment RS

Space 3 2 1

Base row

Hem backing RS

Hem WS

Stitch 3 2 1

2. Trace a line from st on needle to 2nd row above ribbing to find base row.

Turning the hem

Base row—2nd row of stockinette

Garment RS

Turning row

Hem RS

3. Fold hem flap up to base row. Bring yarn needle threaded with waste yarn out of first space on base row.

4. Slip first hem st pwise to yarn needle. Reinsert needle in same space on base row.

5. Needle goes behind next st on base row and comes out next space; repeat until all sts are on waste yarn—yarn needle to back.

Hem sts on waste yarn

Base row—between 2 purl ridges

6. Hold both ends of waste yarn and pull it tight to pop hem sts to wrong side.

7. Slip sts from waste yarn to double-pointed needle; remove waste yarn.

8. Using project yarn tail, bind off hem sts on inside of garment.

or so you can knit them in the other direction—you just undo the crochet chain.

Try out a PDS hem on a swatch of about 25 stitches, as shown in the drawings at left. Begin with crochet provisional cast-on, and leave a tail of the knitting yarn about five times as long as the piece's width. Work an inch or so of reverse stockinette for the hem. Change to needles that are two or three sizes smaller and work one row for turning (purl on the knit side or knit on the purl side). Then work k1, p1 rib for one row shorter than the reverse stockinette area. I discovered using ribbing as a backing in Maggie Righetti's *Knitting in Plain English* (New York: St. Martin's Press, 1986). The rib on smaller needles makes a nicely firm but stretchy backing for your hem so it will lie smoothly without flaring, and it also helps you distinguish the hem and body fabric. Change back to the larger needles, and work several inches of stockinette.

Now you're ready to turn up the hem, as shown at far left. Undo the crochet chain and put the cast-on loops on a double-pointed needle. There will be only 24 stitches because the cast-on makes you lose a half stitch at each edge. To find the base row (the second row of stockinette above the ribbed section where you'll pull the hem stitches through) and to see how the stitches on the needle and the spaces in the base row align, trace along a column of stitches from one of the stitches on the double-pointed needle. You'll notice that this line includes a half-knit/half-purl stitch in the ribbing section. It's important to work a PDS hem into the spaces directly above the loops on the needle—these spaces will be between stitches on the base row, which compensates for the lost cast-on stitch.

Now you're ready to PDS, as shown in the three right-hand drawings at left. Drop the project yarn and thread a yarn needle with waste yarn about twice as long as the swatch's width. There is no need to pull the waste yarn all the way through the work. As a short length of waste yarn fills up with stitches, tug on it, but hold both ends so no stitches drop off. This will pop the stitches through to the wrong side of the knitting. When you've transferred all the stitches to the waste yarn, count to make sure you haven't lost any, and check that no extra strands have found their way onto the waste yarn. All the stitches should be just about perpendicular to the waste yarn. Anything at a different angle probably results from splitting the yarn and does not belong there. Also check that all the stitches have been pulled through on

Illustrations by Phoebe Gaughan

the same row. This is easy to see on the purl side because the waste yarn with the stitches will sit comfortably between two of the purl ridges. Put a smaller size knitting needle through the stitches and remove the waste yarn. Finally, use the cast-on tail and the project-size needle to bind off the hem stitches. Don't bind off too tightly. If you're knitting in the round or PDSing in the middle of an area (decorative effects), you'll need to bring the tail through the space adjacent to the first stitch to bind off with it. Secure the last stitch. That's all there is to it.

Any errors that you find can be corrected as you work off the stitches on the needle. Simply work up to the offending stitch, slip it off the knitting needle, pop it out to the other side of the fabric, and pull it through the correct space with a crochet hook. Then put it back onto the knitting needle and continue. Work twisted stitches through the back loops or reposition them.

It's a good idea to put down a bottom-up hem as soon as you've completed an inch or two beyond the base row. If the flap is too short, you'll find out before too much of the project is completed. Of course, if the flap is in stockinette stitch, you can lengthen it by knitting from the invisible cast-on.

PDSing a patch pocket

In a bottom-up hem, the PDS loops are formed by an invisible cast-on (they're the end of the knitting in a top-down hem), and the spaces occur between knit stitches. But loops can also be formed at the sides of a project by making a *small loop selvage*, described below, and a space can be any place a yarn needle can go. Thus, it's possible to develop a wide range of uses for PDS.

One of the most satisfying applications for PDS is attaching patch pockets, because the sides and bottom of the pocket can be made to blend imperceptibly into the fabric of the garment, as shown in the photo on p. 87. You can make the bottom loops of the pocket with an invisible cast-on. The side loops are made by enlarging the nubs that occur at the sides of a knitted piece. This small loop selvage is very easy to do. Simply catch a bundle of waste yarn along the side just as you begin each row. The bundle will capture loops for PDSing and will ensure that all the loops are the same size.

Make two bundles of waste yarn (one for each side) by knotting several strands together top and bottom. Determine the number of strands you need by swatching, (four times the thickness of your project yarn is a good rule of thumb). The bundles should be a little longer than the length of the pocket.

Place a bundle close to the selvage in front of the project yarn at the beginning of the first row. Before you work the first stitch, catch the project yarn around the bundle along the edge. Catch the second bundle along the other edge at the beginning of the next row. Repeat all the way up the sides of the pocket, pulling the bundles up bit by bit. When you are done, insert a needle into the loops on the bundle yarn, as shown below, unknot one end of the bundle, and remove it. PDS the loops on the bottom and both sides through the garment, bottom first. Since there is only one side loop for every two rows on the pocket, PDS these loops through every other row on the garment. Also, bring both yarn tails through to the inside of the garment. The selvage loops get lost very easily, so if you need to undo a PDS join, be careful to rip out loop by loop, picking up each loop as you come to it.

There are several options for binding off, depending on the size of the selvage loops. If the loops are fairly small, just use the final tail to bind off all the loops around the three sides. But if they're very large, use an *unworked bind-off*, which is about as simple as a bind-off can get. You work it without any yarn, so to be able to secure the final loop, you must work the bind-off toward a free yarn tail or stitch it down with a separate piece of yarn. Here's how you do it:

1. Slip two stitches purlwise from the left to the right needle.

2. Pass the first stitch over the second and off the right needle.

3. Slip the next stitch to the right needle, and pass the first stitch over it.

When only one loop remains on the right needle, secure it with the nearby tail.

I often use a combination bind-off on pockets so that the corners will be very neat on the inside. I use unworked bind-off on the first side, bind off the bottom normally with the cast-on tail, and then bind off the second side with unworked bind-off. Be sure to finish the tails, too, by drawing each through a loop as you come to it. □

Paula Levy of East Windsor, NJ, is an associate member of the Professional Knitwear Designers Guild and has completed the master knitting program of The Knitting Guild of America.

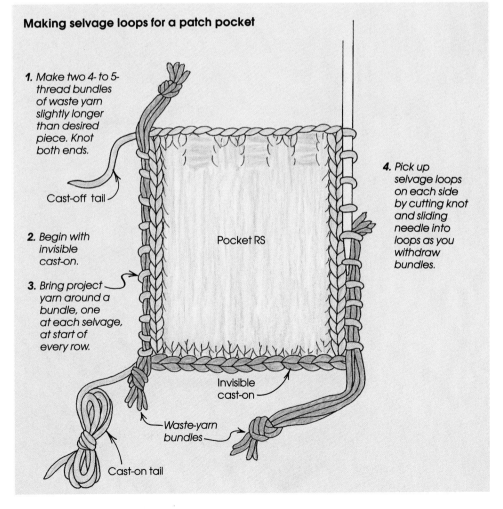

Making selvage loops for a patch pocket

1. Make two 4- to 5-thread bundles of waste yarn slightly longer than desired piece. Knot both ends.

Cast-off tail

2. Begin with invisible cast-on.

3. Bring project yarn around a bundle, one at each selvage, at start of every row.

Pocket RS

4. Pick up selvage loops on each side by cutting knot and sliding needle into loops as you withdraw bundles.

Invisible cast-on

Waste-yarn bundles

Cast-on tail

Cardigan Borders
Knit them now or pick 'em up later

by Pam Allen

a cardigan border is practical. It keeps the edges of your sweater from drooping and provides a place for buttons and buttonholes. It's also a design element. Like any good conclusion—whether simple or fancy—a cardigan border sums up your sweater design.

There are two basic ways to work a cardigan band; whether you pick up or knit in will depend on your design (see sketches, p. 91). For details on each method, see pp. 91-93. If you knit the bands in when you knit the fronts of the sweater, you'll have to do more planning and experimenting to ensure the desired look and correct dimensions. A garter-stitch band is best knit in.

Picked-up bands, which you work after completing the fronts, give you more leeway for later planning; and a vertical picked-up band, which runs parallel to the front edge, looks just like a knit-in band. I often use a horizontal picked-up band, which is set perpendicular to the front edge, because I like the way it looks. Picked-up bands are best for V necks because they go all the way around the sweater's front opening. In this case, you can pick up all the stitches on both fronts and the neck edge and knit a continuous horizontal band. If you want to do a stranded, patterned band, pick it up and knit horizontally.

(continued on p. 91)

Cardigans are practical and fun to make once you lick the border problem. Pam Allen worked the child's sweater with a knit-in garter-stitch border. The adult's features a 2 x 2 picked-up horizontal border. (Photo by Susan Kahn)

Calculating front and border widths

Whether you knit the band into the body of the sweater or add it later, you must figure out the width of each front piece, taking into account the width of the border. Your goal is for the center of the border to fall at the center front. For this to happen, each front will measure half the width of the back plus half the width of the border.

Having determined the stitch gauges for the body and border fabrics, figure out the number of stitches in the back and the number in the border. Then subtract half the number of border stitches from half the number of back stitches—the front. For a knit-in band, you cast on the full number of border stitches, plus the remaining front stitches. The pattern stitches will be apportioned so you have complete borders on each piece (top drawing below). For picked-up bands, you just cast on the front stitches, minus the band stitches, adding a seam stitch if desired.

Making the border lie flat

Ribbing, seed stitch and its variations, and garter stitch are the most familiar noncurling stitches, but check stitch-pattern books for others. When you're swatching border patterns, pay attention to the outer edges of your swatch. That's how the edge of your band will look. It may need a selvage stitch or stitches to look neat. For a garter-stitch border, slip the edge stitch knitwise when it begins a row, and knit it when it's last.

For a ribbed knit-in border (k1, p1), allow an odd number of stitches for the band. On the right side, the stitch next to the cardigan body should be purled. The edge should end in k2. Work a chain selvage in the edge stitch as follows: On the right side, slip the edge stitch knitwise when it begins the row, and knit it when it ends the row. On wrong-side rows, slip the edge stitch purlwise at the beginning of the row, and purl it at the end of the row. The chain selvage will curl a bit to the wrong side, leaving a

Making picked-up borders

Work picked-up bands after you've completed the fronts and back and sewn the shoulders together. Picking up a complete front border and knitting perpendicular to the sweater front, you form a horizontal border. If you pick up each front edge stitch as you come to it and work parallel to the front, you produce a vertical border. Don't cast on the border stitches when you knit the fronts; add 1 st extra at each center-front edge for a "seam."

When knitting the fronts, I prefer to work the edge stitches snugly, rather than work a selvage of some sort. Pull gently on the yarn after you've knit the edge stitch and inserted the needle into the next stitch. This way, you'll be able to count the stitches that you'll be picking up from much more easily than if you've skipped one every other row.

Once you've completed the fronts and joined them to the back at the shoulders, but before you begin picking up stitches, you'll need to decide how the front bands will meet the neckband—a moot point if your cardigan is a V neck, in which case, the band is continuous.

If the border is to be interrupted, the neckband can stop short of the front borders, letting them form an uninterrupted line up the front of the sweater (my preference); or it can cover the top edges of the front bands. For uninterrupted front borders, pick up and knit the neckband first. When you pick up stitches for the border fronts, pick up at the center-front edges of the neckband too. If the neckband is to cover the top borders, knit the front borders first, and then pick up along the neck edge and border tops.

Pick-up ratio, horizontal border

The crucial consideration for any horizontal picked-up border is the ratio of stitches picked up for the border to rows in the sweater body. If too many are picked up, the border will be wavy; too few, and it will pull up. There's no hard-and-fast rule for this. Many factors will determine the right proportion: needle size, weight of yarn, final look desired, etc.

A standard rule of thumb for stockinette fabric is to pick up 2 sts every 3 rows. This is generally fine for a stockinette band knit on slightly smaller needles. If you're picking up a garter-stitch border on a garter-stitch body, pick up 1 st for every 2 rows on a slightly smaller needle. But once you

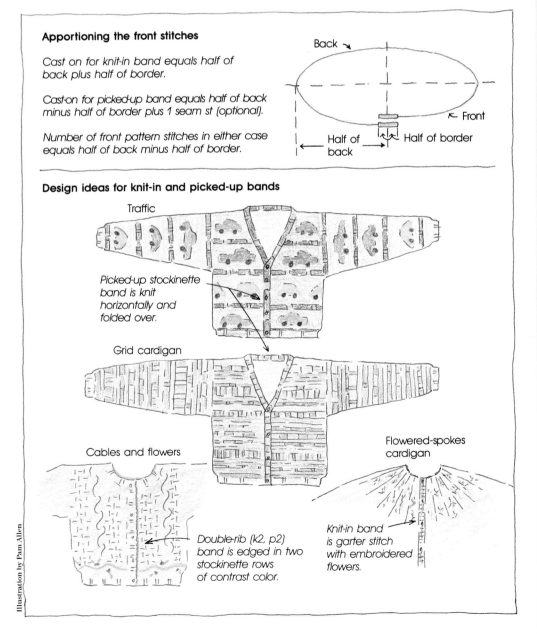

Apportioning the front stitches

Cast on for knit-in band equals half of back plus half of border.

Cast-on for picked-up band equals half of back minus half of border plus 1 seam st (optional).

Number of front pattern stitches in either case equals half of back minus half of border.

Back

Front

Half of back   Half of border

Design ideas for knit-in and picked-up bands

Traffic

Picked-up stockinette band is knit horizontally and folded over.

Grid cardigan

Cables and flowers

Double-rib (k2, p2) band is edged in two stockinette rows of contrast color.

Flowered-spokes cardigan

Knit-in band is garter stitch with embroidered flowers.

Illustration by Pam Allen

move away from these fabrics, you'll have to experiment on a swatch or your sweater front before starting. When I'm adding a ribbed band, I usually use needles three to five sizes smaller than those I used on the sweater body and often pick up 4 or 5 sts before I skip a row; sometimes I pick up 1 st for every row.

To calculate your pick-up ratio for a horizontal border, knit a 4-in.-wide swatch of the border pattern on the size needles you think work best. Count the number of stitches in 3 in. Then count the number of rows in 3 in. of the sweater body, at least 2 in. from the edge. Use small safety pins to mark 3 in. worth of rows on the front edge, and pick up the number of stitches for 3 in. of border between those pins, skipping evenly.

Whatever your ratio, you may have to fudge the total number of stitches to be picked up to accommodate a ribbed or patterned border. A k2, p2 rib needs a multiple of 4 sts to come out even. If you want it to begin and end k2, pick up a multiple of 4 sts, plus 2 sts.

Working a horizontal border
The most standard type of horizontal border is ribbed. You can jazz up a ribbed border by working stripes or edging it in a different color (work the last row and bind off in the new color). Another way to edge the border is to work a small roll or a picot bind-off. For a small roll, finish off the border with several rows of reverse stockinette. You can find a variety of interesting bind-offs in Montse Stanley's *The Handknitter's Handbook* (Sterling, 1986).

If you want a smoother, less sporty look than ribbing may allow, consider a stockinette band knit to twice the required depth, folded over, and sewn down. This makes an unobtrusive finish in a solid color, or it can look like a colorful ribbon if worked in a Fair Isle pattern in several colors. For a picot turning edge on your stockinette border, work k1, yo, k2tog, across the turning row on the right side. Otherwise, work a purl row on the right side at the fold line for a crisp edge. You can also work a picked-up border in any of the noncurling stitches.

When picking up stitches, insert your needle from the right side through the space between the edge stitch and the next one in, catch the strand of yarn you'll be working with, and pull a new loop through (top photo). Work the tail in later. Repeat up the edge, skipping rows as calculated.

To work a continuous band on a crewneck sweater, pick up all the stitches from the bottom of one front to the bottom of the other on a long circular needle. You must use a pair of circular needles as if they were straight needles because no straight needle is long enough to hold so many stitches. You could even pick up all the stitches around the front, bottom, and neck edges of the cardigan and work a continuous, circular band around the perimeter of the sweater. In either case, you must miter the corners—where the front band meets the neck and the lower front corners (on a perimeter band)—by working double increases at each corner, every other row or round. Plan the buttonhole placement after 2 rows. When the border is wide enough, bind off in pattern. If you're knitting a doubled border, work a purl turning row at the midpoint; then work the facing side, making double decreases at the corners. Sew the doubled band to the wrong side of the sweater 1 st at a time straight from the needle.

Working a vertical border
You work a vertical border as you attach it to the sweater front. On a slightly smaller needle, cast on stitches the width of the desired border and work the border from bottom to top, picking up 1 st from the front edge on each row. You work off 1 st or loop from the front edge of the sweater together with the sweater edge stitch of the border on each row. Even though you're alternating between right and wrong sides, the stitch you pick up from the front edge of the sweater is always taken from the right side of the sweater. You often work the same number of rows in the border as are on the front, but you need to scrutinize the pick-up after a few inches to make sure the border is hanging properly.

If you're working a 1 x 1 ribbed border, cast on an odd number of stitches the width you want the border to be. This allows an extra stitch at the open edge for a chain selvage and ensures that the stitch next to the sweater will be purled on the right side. Let's say that you've cast on 9 border sts. For the right front, work as follows (see bottom three photos at right):

Row 1 (RS): Slip 1 border st knitwise, (k1, p1)3x, k1, yarn to front, slip last stitch on LHN purlwise to RHN. With RHN, pick up 1 st in from edge stitch. Slip picked-up stitch and last border stitch to LHN. P2tog, yarn to back. With RHN, pick up loop on next row up of sweater edge. Turn work.

Row 2 (WS): K2tog, (p1, k1)3x, p2. Repeat these 2 rows up sweater front. For left front, begin attaching band on second row, working 1 wrong-side row on border stitches only first. –P.A. ⇨

To pick up stitches for a horizontal border, insert the needle from the right side into the space between the edge stitch and the second stitch and pull up a loop from behind.

For a picked-up vertical border, work across the right side of the border stitches (row 1) and slip the last stitch purlwise with the yarn in front. Pick up the next front stitch, and p2tog.

Then bring the yarn to the back and pick up the next front stitch from the right side before turning the work.

Turn the work to the wrong side (row 2). K2tog. Then work to the end of the border stitches and turn. Repeat rows 1 and 2.

well-shaped knit stitch at the edge. Some border patterns, like those done in seed stitch, may look better without a selvage stitch, but be careful to work the edge stitches with a firm tension to keep them even.

If you want to knit a stockinette band, you'll have to knit a facing for it; otherwise, it will curl in. After figuring the band width in stitches for a knit-in band, add twice the required number of band stitches, plus 1 st in the middle for the turning row, to the front stitches. On right-side rows, slip the turning stitch purlwise; on wrong-side rows, purl it. For picked-up bands, knit the band to its desired width. Then work a purl row on the right side, and knit the facing the same width as the band.

Neckline shaping

The way you work the neckline decreases determines how easily you can pick up stitches later from around the neck edge. Work all the decreases 1 st in from the edge. For visible ones that slant in the same direction as the neckline curve, work SSK (slip 2 sts knitwise, 1 st at a time; insert the LHN, and knit them together) on the right front, and k2tog on the left front.

I get a better curve if I bind off, rather than decrease, for the front-neck stitches. Often, on the rows after the initial center-front bind-off, I bind off 3 sts (slipping the first stitch), then 2 sts, then 1 st. I keep binding off 1 st at the neck edge every other row until I have the same number of stitches left as on the back shoulder. I prefer to bind off the back-neck stitches, rather than put them on a holder, as they won't stretch, and the band will have more definition.

Buttonholes

If possible, work your cardigan's button band first so you can experiment with button placement before committing yourself to buttonholes. When picking up a continuous horizontal border around a V-neck cardigan, work two rows of the border first, and plan your buttonholes when you can see how the knit and purl stitches fall. I like to nestle buttonholes in the purl troughs, where they virtually disappear. See the buttonholes on the facing page.

A good buttonhole is unobtrusive. It's neat, and it fits into the band, disturbing the pattern as little as possible. Its edges should be firm enough to hold the button in place and not stretch over time. There are many ways to knit buttonholes, although most commercial patterns instruct you only to cast off so many stitches on one row and knit them back on in the next. Directions for other types are on p. 94.

Buttons and buttonholes can be evenly spaced, or they can be grouped in clusters of two or three for design interest, particularly nice with small buttons on a narrow band. On a wide-ribbed waistband that wants to pull open, put more buttons there. Generally, buttons should be positioned ½ in. to 1 in. from the top and bottom edges.

If you center your buttonhole and button horizontally in their bands, the buttonhole band will slide away from the center until the button catches in the corner of the buttonhole. Start the buttonhole off-center, closer to the sweater front, and the button will stay nestled in the buttonhole corner, at the center of the band. Or sew the button off-center, closer to the sweater front.

For a fold-over band, you need two buttonholes for each opening—one buttonhole on the right side and one on the facing. To finish buttonholes, baste them closed with sewing thread, lining up knit stitches and purl troughs. Then steam them lightly from the wrong side. For a fold-over band, baste the right-side buttonhole closed, and steam it lightly. When it's dry, remove the basting thread, and with matching sewing thread, sew the facing carefully to the buttonhole on the wrong side of the border.

Buttons

Buttons can make or break your sweater. A very small button on a large, bulky sweater can be as jarring to the eye as an oversized button on a dainty sweater. If you can't find the perfect button, consider making your own, as described in "Buttoning it up" on p. 94.

If a button has no shank, don't sew it flush to your sweater; the buttonhole band will pucker when buttoned. Insert something like a matchstick between the button and the sweater when sewing the button on. After sewing, remove the separator and wind your thread or yarn around the shank that you've made to strengthen it.

If you're sewing a button on a lace sweater without much to grab, put a small, clear button back to back on the wrong side and sew the two buttons together simultaneously. The clear button will anchor the outside one. Work a shank if necessary.

Pam Allen of Camden, ME, is a knitwear designer who sells her handmade and machine-made sweaters in a local gallery.

Making knit-in borders

Designate a number of stitches on the center-front edge of each front piece as "band" stitches, and work them in whatever pattern your border calls for, row by row, as you knit the front pieces.

Preventing a loose border

The main drawback to working a knit-in border is that if you knit it on the same size needles as the rest of the sweater, it may be too loose. One remedy is to work short rows (2 fewer rows on the border than on the body) every 3 or 4 in.

Starting at the side edge, work across to the border. Leaving the yarn where it is, slip the first border stitch to the RHN, and bring the yarn to the other side of the

knitting. Return the slipped stitch to the LHN, and the yarn is wrapped around it to prevent a hole. Turn, and work back across the front to the side edge. On the return row, work the slipped stitch together with its wrap as you continue across the border.

You can also ensure a firm edge by working the border stitches on smaller double-pointeds. Knit the border on them, and leave the stitches on them. Knit the rest of the front on the large needles. Each time you reach the border, switch to the small needles. Pull a little on the yarn at the junction of the two needles so the join is neat. If you knit the border in garter stitch, you can probably

use the body needles all the way across, as garter stitch tends to draw up on its own.

When you reach the neckline shaping, leave the border stitches on holders and complete the fronts.

Working the neckband

After you've completed the fronts and joined them to the back at the shoulders, transfer the right-front border stitches to the needle you plan to use for the neckband, and pick up stitches around the neck edge, ending with the left-front border. On the curves or diagonal edges, pick up stitches, skipping every third or fourth stitch, whichever looks better. Pick up every stitch along the back-neck

edge. Make sure the total number of stitches you pick up is a multiple of your border pattern; e.g., if you're knitting a 1 x 1 ribbed border with a purl as the last stitch on the sweater side, you must pick up an odd number of stitches to keep the ribs in the neckband consistent with those in the border. Work the band the desired depth, and bind off in pattern.

If the band isn't ribbed, working a decrease on each side of the shoulder seam every other row helps the neckband lie flat. If you're knitting the neckband double, increase at the shoulder seams every other row on the facing side to correspond to the decreases on the right side. –P.A.

Buttoning it up

Buttonholes

To practice making buttonholes, cast on 20 sts in sport- or medium-weight yarn. Using needles two sizes smaller than for the body of the sweater, work k1, p1 rib for about 1 in. Mark the right side of your swatch, and work all the buttonholes from this side.

Eyelet buttonhole—Good for small buttons, particularly on children's sweaters (see first photo below). For a small eyelet (1 row), work k1, p1 for 9 sts, ending k1 (buttonhole will be in purl trough). Yarn to the front (makes an automatic yo), k2tog. Finish p1, k1 to end. A large eyelet takes 3 rows.
Row 1: Work k1, p1 for 9 sts, ending k1. Yo twice. K2tog, p1, k1 to end of row.
Row 2: Rib to yo's, ending p1. Knit first yo, drop second yo, p1, k1 to end of row.
Row 3: Rib to buttonhole and purl into hole below. Complete row.

Vertical slit (even number of rows)—Good for any size button. The chain selvages along the slit roll to the back, making it blend perfectly into the ribbing. When working this buttonhole in stockinette (second photo), don't work increase, which is there only to align the knit ribs.
Row 1: Work k1, p1 for 10 sts, ending p1. *With separate strand of yarn*, purl into stitch below next stitch (increase 1 st), k1, p1 to end of row.
Row 2: K1, p1 to buttonhole, ending k1 in increase stitch. Pick up original strand of yarn, insert RHN knitwise into first stitch, pull yarn gently, and slip stitch to RHN. P1, k1 to end of row.
Row 3: K1, p1 to buttonhole, ending p1. With second strand of yarn and yarn in front, slip first stitch purlwise, pulling gently on yarn. K1, p1 to end of row.
Rows 4 and 5: Repeat rows 2 and 3 as many times as needed.
Row 6: K1, p1 to within 1 st of opening. To close buttonhole from WS, k2tog at top of slit. Rib to end of row. Cut separate strand and darn in ends.

Self-reinforcing buttonhole, horizontal (1 row)—Works for any size button. It looks different, but equally neat, worked from the wrong side. Worked on a horizontal rib, it's vertical (third photo).
Step 1. K1, p1 for 8 sts, ending p1.
Step 2. Slip next stitch purlwise, yarn to back, slip 1 st more purlwise to RHN.
Step 3. Pass first slipped stitch over second (1 st bound-off). Slipping stitches from LHN to RHN, continue binding off—total of 5 sts.
Step 4. Slip last bound-off stitch from RHN to LHN. Turn work.
Step 5. With yarn in back, cast on 6 sts (1 st more than bound-off), using *Cable Cast-On* as follows: Insert RHN between first and second stitches on LHN, and draw through a loop. Slip loop onto LHN (first cast-on stitch). Repeat, inserting RHN between last cast-on stitch and previous stitch. Before putting last cast-on stitch onto LHN, bring yarn to front. Turn work.
Step 6. Slip first stitch from LHN to RHN and pass last cast-on stitch over it. Rib to end of row.

Buttons

There are several ways to make a crocheted button that will match your sweater perfectly. You can crochet a small, stuffed ball (last photo); you can cover a flat button (second photo); or you can work around a small ring. (For a description of ring buttons, see Montse Stanley's *The Handknitter's Handbook* (Sterling, 1986) or Maggie Righetti's *Knitting in Plain English* (St. Martin's, 1986). To get the right effect, play with the directions below, varying hook size and numbers of stitches and rounds.

Ball button— Using a crochet hook several sizes smaller than you'd ordinarily use with your yarn, ch3. Join into ring with slip stitch, ch1.
Round 1: Work 6 sc into ring. Join with slip stitch, ch1.
Round 2: *1 sc in next sc, 2 sc in next sc*. Repeat from *-* around—9 sc. Join, ch1.
Round 3: Work 1 sc in each sc. Join, ch1.
Round 4: Decrease: *Insert hook into next sc, yo, draw loop through; insert hook into next sc, yo and draw loop through; yo and draw loop through all 3 loops on hook.* Continue from *-*, working decreases until opening is almost closed.

Insert a wooden bead (10 mm is a good size), or stuff with yarn. Close opening with more spiral decreases if ball isn't covered, or thread yarn on a tapestry needle and run through remaining sc's to gather up. Cut yarn, pull tail through, and use it to sew on button.

Some yarns will require that you ch2 for the initial ring, some will require 4 ch. You may be able to fit more sc's in the initial ring, maybe fewer. You may not need the even round of sc's. Instead, you may need to decrease on the round immediately following the increase round. If your yarn is too thick, and plied, you may want to work with 1 ply. Cut a 5-ft. length. Clip a clothespin on one end, and separate the plies from the other end.

Flat button—Ch3 and join into ring with a slip stitch, ch1.
Round 1: Work 6 sc into ring, join with slip stitch, ch1.
Round 2: Work 2 sc in each sc—12 sc. Join, ch1.
Round 3: Decrease: Inserting hook into back loops of sc stitches, *insert hook into first sc, yo, and draw loop through; insert hook into next sc, yo, and draw loop through; yo and draw loop through all 3 loops on hook.* Continue from *-*, inserting a flat button the same color as the yarn after the first round. Work decreases until entire button is covered. Cut yarn, pull tail through, and use it to sew on button. Improvise however you wish.—P.A. □

Eyelets are good for small buttons and look neat on a 1 x 1 ribbed band or in the purl ribs of a 2 x 2 ribbing. They're unobtrusive but not very tailored-looking on stockinette.

Vertical slits are perfect for large buttons on a vertically picked-up 1 x 1 ribbed border, or as shown here, on stockinette. You make the button by crocheting over a flat button.

Self-reinforcing buttonholes can lie horizontally or vertically. Worked over an odd number of stitches on a 1 x 1 ribbed border, they fall neatly between purl troughs.

Crocheted buttons are fun and easy to make, and they match your sweater perfectly. To make a ball button, use a smaller-than-normal hook, and insert a wooden bead.

Index

If you enjoyed this book, you'll love our magazine.

A year's subscription to *Threads* brings you the kind of hands-on information you found in this book, and much more. In issue after issue—six times a year—you'll discover articles on sewing, quilting, knitting and other needlecrafts. Artists and professionals share their best techniques and trade secrets with you. With detailed illustrations and full-color photographs that bring each project to life, *Threads* will inspire you to create your best work ever!

To subscribe, just fill out one of the attached subscription cards or call us toll free at 1-800-888-8286.

The Taunton Press Guarantee

If you are not completely satisfied you may cancel at any time and we'll immediately refund your payment in full.

Taunton
BOOKS & VIDEOS
for fellow enthusiasts

The Taunton Press 63 S. Main Street, P.O. Box 5506, Newtown, CT 06470-5506

Threads

Use this card to subscribe to *Threads* or to request information about other Taunton Press magazines, books and videos.

☐ 1 year (6 issues) for just $28—over 15% off the newsstand price. Outside the U.S. $34/year (U.S. funds, please. Canadian residents: GST included)

☐ 2 years (12 issues) for just $48—27% off the newsstand price. Outside the U.S. $56/year (U.S. funds, please. Canadian residents: GST included)

Name _____

Address _____

City _____

State _____ Zip _____

☐ My payment is enclosed.   ☐ Please bill me.
☐ Please send me information about other Taunton Press magazines, books and videos. (BBBS)

I'm interested in:
1 ☐ sewing   5 ☐ knitting
2 ☐ embroidery   6 ☐ quilting
3 ☐ woodworking   7 ☐ home building
4 ☐ gardening   8 ☐ other

BTH6

Threads

Use this card to subscribe to *Threads* or to request information about other Taunton Press magazines, books and videos.

☐ 1 year (6 issues) for just $28—over 15% off the newsstand price. Outside the U.S. $34/year (U.S. funds, please. Canadian residents: GST included)

☐ 2 years (12 issues) for just $48—27% off the newsstand price. Outside the U.S. $56/year (U.S. funds, please. Canadian residents: GST included)

Name _____

Address _____

City _____

State _____ Zip _____

☐ My payment is enclosed.   ☐ Please bill me.
☐ Please send me information about other Taunton Press magazines, books and videos. (BBBS)

I'm interested in:
1 ☐ sewing   5 ☐ knitting
2 ☐ embroidery   6 ☐ quilting
3 ☐ woodworking   7 ☐ home building
4 ☐ gardening   8 ☐ other

BTH6

Taunton
BOOKS & VIDEOS
for fellow enthusiasts

NO POSTAGE
NECESSARY
IF MAILED
IN THE
UNITED STATES

BUSINESS REPLY MAIL
FIRST CLASS MAIL   PERMIT NO.19   NEWTOWN, CT

POSTAGE WILL BE PAID BY ADDRESSEE

Threads®
63 SOUTH MAIN STREET
PO BOX 5506
NEWTOWN CT 06470-9976

Taunton
BOOKS & VIDEOS
for fellow enthusiasts

NO POSTAGE
NECESSARY
IF MAILED
IN THE
UNITED STATES

BUSINESS REPLY MAIL
FIRST CLASS MAIL   PERMIT NO.19   NEWTOWN, CT

POSTAGE WILL BE PAID BY ADDRESSEE

Threads®
63 SOUTH MAIN STREET
PO BOX 5506
NEWTOWN CT 06470-9976